a family island

by
H. Shaw McCutcheon

and rush through, the walls barely an arm's length away on either side of the boat. Suddenly the visitors would be gliding across a glassy lagoon to a concrete pier jutting out from a small beach. Behind the pier was a forest of palm and casuarina trees. The only sound was the low drone of the distant surf; otherwise there was total silence. For many it was like a time warp, a looking-glass passage into a tranquil world distinct from the hubbub of everyday life on the Outside.

The island sat on an east-west axis for three and a half miles and was shaped roughly like a spoon, with the wide end of the spoon on the eastern end enclosing a lagoon a half-mile long by a quarter mile wide. With one exception, all the houses and activities were centered around the lagoon. The heart of the island was the north side, the chief feature of which was a hill about 40 feet at its highest point. The sturdy Main House, constructed in the late 1800s, was located here, protected from the elements by a cliff just to the north and twin rows of carefully clipped casuarinas on the other three sides.

The interior was a garden of carefully manicured palms and flowering plants laid out on a bed of white sand and connected by a system of concrete pathways. Down the hill to the east of the Main House were two guest cottages and a rigid canvas-lined tent culled from an African safari. A path went past the guest cottages to the South Beach, a small beach on the southeast end of the island, which sported its own dressing house and which the family used for years as a place for nude bathing.

To the west of the Main House the path meandered

around the lagoon, past the caretakers' homes, to a "T". The path going left went to the stone watchtower, which my grandfather, John T. McCutcheon, had built next to the cut on a whim back in the 1920s. The path heading to the right went to the Custom House, a drawbridge on the south side which was for decades the main entrance to the island.

Part of the essential charm of Salt Cay was in the primitive living conditions. Fresh water was supplied by a system of cisterns scattered about the island. Everyone bathed in the ocean or with buckets of fresh water lifted by rope from the cisterns. Holding tanks above the bathrooms, fed by hand pumps drawing water from the cisterns (and later from salt water wells), supplied the water for toilets. Fresh water was precious and used sparingly.

There was never any electricity, so light came from kerosene lamps. Bright "Aladdin" lamps, which gave off the light of a 20-watt bulb, were used to read with; hurricane lamps were used everywhere else. Flashlights were de rigeur, and in later years some family members introduced the

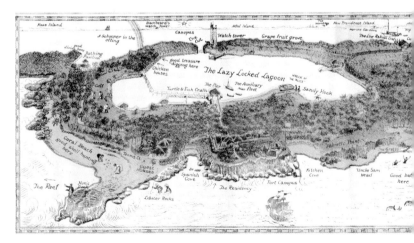

battery-powered radio, which — to the dismay of a few — provided news of the Outside World. For years the kitchen was powered with kerosene-fueled refrigerators and stoves; later we switched to propane. Without electricity there was no reason to buy a radiotelephone.

The lack of communications became a humorous nuisance in the 1970s when Caspar Weinberger, who was then Richard Nixon's Secretary of Defense, visited the place for a few days as the guest of my uncle, John McCutcheon. Whenever Nixon wanted to reach Weinberger the White House had to call a local marina in Nassau, who would send out a boat to the island and take Weinberger back to Nassau to return the call. Nixon was most likely not impressed.

Today the island has been converted into a major commercial enterprise, and the old way of life on the place has gone the way of the mansions at Newport and the other relics of a less egalitarian era. The same storm that inspired the book and movie "The Perfect Storm" cut the island in two at the northwestern corner of the lagoon. Three enormous

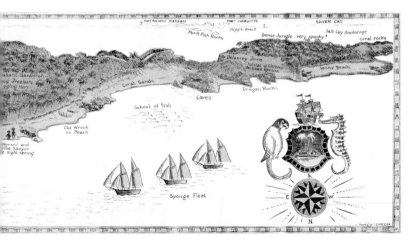

30-foot waves did the job in one single night. Elsewhere, the south beach has disappeared, replaced by a major tourist attraction with dolphins. Here, too, the island has been sliced up, this time by man. The Main House, which after a century finally began to decay, has been torn down, leaving only the kitchen oven and the foundations at the top of the hill. The cut has been widened from 14 to almost 50 feet to accommodate the tourist boats, and down beyond the lagoon at the west end of the island there are other tourist facilities, a helicopter landing pad and a second landing area.

Here and there, however, evidence remains of our six decades of ownership: the tower still commands the entrance; the two guest cottages have been converted to staff bungalows; the caretaker's home has been painted with bright pastels; and the Custom House still stands. The forest of palms — we planted 200 new trees every year — still provides a shady canopy over the interior. The Balinese statue my grandfather brought from Asia, called Bali-Ghit-Ghit, is still perched in the midst of a small courtyard down from the Main House that we used for candlelit dinners.

The island has been renamed for marketing purposes "Blue Lagoon Island."

It is estimated that close to 300,000 tourists visit the place every year to enjoy the palm forests, the quiet beaches, the dolphins and the hammocks. This book is intended to place into context much of what they see, how one family of relatively modest means found themselves owning and maintaining one of the classic dreams everyone aspires to — a private family island.

chapter one
the honeymoon

A surge of adrenalin rushed through John T. McCutcheon as he stepped off the ship onto Nassau's busy wharf. A lifelong dream of strolling about his very own private island was almost a reality, and the exhilaration that had consumed him since he signed the purchase papers a few months before had now turned into almost unbearable impatience at the thought that only a brief sailboat ride stood between him and that dream.

He grabbed Evelyn's hand and pushed his way through the crowded streets to the *Alice*, the yawl that had come with the island and which would take him out there. Having never actually seen the place he had no idea what to expect, and his excitement was tinged with trepidation at the possibility that what he had bought by mail would be no more than a limestone rock, a beach and perhaps a tree or two on it.

John T. removed his straw hat and frowned at the thought. He was a slight man with dark, swept-back hair parted down the middle in the fashion of the times. His sharp, angled features were dominated by a large beaked nose and oversized ears that made him, if not handsome, at least distinctive. Dark eyes peered out from deep sockets, but they twinkled when he smiled. He was 46 years old and had just married Evelyn, a young, blue-eyed woman exactly half his age who had first fallen in love with him when she was only five years old and he was a famous foreign correspondent for a large metropolitan newspaper. Their visit to this mysterious island called Salt Cay on the map was the last stop of their two-month honeymoon.

For many, the idea of owning an exotic island where one can escape the cacophonous hubbub of daily living and become master of his own miniature kingdom remains one of those hopeless, Mittyesque dreams sandwiched in between worries about the job and making enough money to pay the bills and send the children to college. But for John T., the dream was an obsession, and for years he had searched throughout the globe for an island he could afford. His fame around the Chicago area had grown, as he became one of the Chicago Tribune's chief foreign correspondents and the newspaper's only political cartoonist. Along with the fame came increasing fortune in a larger salary, but money was never John T.'s primary concern. Fortunately, his salary permitted him an occasional extravagance.

One spring afternoon in 1916, while America was preparing to go to war, Charles Atkinson rushed over to John T.'s office at the Tribune and showed him a small advertisement offering this island in the Bahamas for sale. Atkinson, a close friend who had been to Nassau before and had heard John T. speak often of his dream, said the place fit his specifications. The cartoonist read and re-read the ad. It didn't say much, just that it was close to Nassau, had a lagoon, a few houses, some beaches and palm trees.

But John T. knew it was in the heart of the pirate belt, where only a couple of hundred years before pirates and buccaneers had cavorted with impunity in what was then a wide-open Nassau. As a boy growing up near the banks of the muddy Wabash River in 19th century Indiana, John T. had been fascinated with tales of seafaring rogues, desert islands and buried treasure, and this island was smack-dab in the middle of all that history.

It was all John T. needed to know, and sight unseen he purchased the island by mail and cable from the estate of a man named, oddly, Van Winkle, a New Jersey manufacturer who had recently died. The price was a suspiciously low $17,500. But that, John T. figured, could be because most people's thoughts were riveted on the impending war, and the demand for islands was about as high as hillside lots on the moon.

A few months after he purchased the island John T. married Evelyn Shaw, the daughter of one of Chicago's most noted architects, Howard Van Doren Shaw. Indeed, he had known Evelyn almost all her life. Atkinson first introduced John T. to the Shaw family in Lake Forest when he was employed as an illustrator and foreign correspondent for the Chicago Record. His main assignment was to travel all over the world covering wars, and whenever he returned to Chicago he would visit the Shaws and describe his adventures to the family. Evelyn, who was then only five years old, would sit at his feet in front of the fireplace and listen in awed silence. By the time she was seven she decided she would have to marry this tall, handsome man. John T. was oblivious to the moonings of this precocious child, as he was preoccupied with other matters. But that didn't stop Evelyn from dreaming of ways to snare him, smiling sweetly and complimenting him on his cartoons whenever he passed through. But by the time she went away to college at Bryn Mawr she had about given up, forlornly telling her classmates she would probably never marry, because the only man she was interested in wasn't a likely candidate.

By pure coincidence, as John T. was negotiating the purchase of the island, he encountered the now-grown Evelyn by chance at a Military Preparedness parade in downtown Chicago. The chance meeting quickly blossomed into a heady romance, culminating in a marriage proposal several months later.

Salt Cay seemed an ideal place for a honeymoon. The marriage of one of the city's most eligible bachelors to the daughter of a famous architect, followed by a honeymoon on this man's private Bahamian island, caught the public's imagination, and the newspapers throughout the country gleefully played up the event in long articles and the society columns.

The only flaw in his plan was that John T. still hadn't seen the place, and nobody was telling him very much about it. Atkinson had become mysteriously reticent to describe it, and Van Winkle's widow wasn't much more informative. She sent him only one long letter listing everything but the kitchen sink they'd have to ferry to the place. He pictured themselves stranded on this desert island without water, surrounded by reeking outhouses, swarms of malarial mosquitoes and half-eaten tins of beans, unable to send for help when Evelyn got mauled by a shark. Concerned, he decided to take the long way around, visiting other Caribbean spots before making Nassau their last stop. If it were as bad as he imagined it, at least the entire honeymoon wouldn't have been a waste.

It was not the typical tropical honeymoon tour. The newlyweds were in Jamaica when the United States broke off diplomatic relations with Germany, quartered in a Colon, Panama hotel with the officers of several German ships that had been interned by the warring U.S. government, and toured Costa Rica during one of its frequent revolutions. In Havana they missed the boat to Nassau and used the extra week to cover an uprising in one of the Cuban provinces for the Tribune, returning to Havana by train through a raging forest fire. By the time they reached the Bahamas Atkinson was there waiting for them, but he was even more guarded that usual. As John T. and Evelyn peppered him with questions about the island — their island — Atkinson blithely suggested they have some breakfast first.

Every question was neatly parried with another about their honeymoon, comments about the weather and the European war. John T. had spent two years covering it, but right now he couldn't think of anything more irrelevant to talk about than war. The couple grew more and more dejected — Evelyn grew silent, listlessly pushing her scrambled eggs around the plate — until Atkinson finally leaned back in his chair, pulled out a cigar, and began talking about the island history.

"So you want to know about your island?" he asked

rhetorically. "It's really a pretty nice place right now, but the lagoon — yes, John, there is a lagoon — had been nothing more than a salt marsh a couple of decades ago. That's how it got its name. Pirates and privateers did use the place, but not to bury treasure, just to cull salt from the marsh to preserve their food. They also used the island as a rest stop while they waited for permission to enter Nassau harbor."

Atkinson paused, sipped his rum drink and squinted at the tired couple across from him. He was enjoying the moment. "In 1875 Charles King-Harmon," he continued, "a Brit who was later knighted and became Governor of Cyprus, bought the island from the Crown for only £35. King-Harmon cleared away the undergrowth, planted 5,000 coconut trees and constructed two houses, one for himself and one for his caretaker. King-Harmon had the place for 11 years, when he sold it to a Bahamian, Sir Augustus John Adderley, for £105. Adderley kept it for six years. He didn't know what to do with it until two Americans who wanted to cultivate corn and vegetables offered him £145. The farming effort failed miserably — what the salt air didn't kill the rats ate — and in 1902 they sold it to Abraham Van Winkle for a £10 loss."

Atkinson stopped there, refusing to discuss the island any further. He didn't tell them, for example, how the diminutive Van Winkle lovingly reshaped its contours into a lush tropical paradise. He hired hundreds of laborers from Nassau to manually dredge out the salt marsh and blasted a 14-foot wide cut through a narrow section to the sea. Opposite the cut he constructed a covered concrete pier, and next to the pier built two large fish "crawls," which were used to store live trap-caught fish until it was time to eat them.

Using tough virgin pine imported from Nova Scotia he erected two guesthouses, enlarged King-Harmon's house on top of the highest hill and constructed a two-room bathhouse on a small beach on the island's southeast end. Then he connected all the buildings and beaches with over a mile of meandering concrete paths and lined them with flowering plants to add dashes of red, white and purple to the verdant landscape. Seven cisterns, capable of containing 30,000 gallons of fresh water, were dug underground and hooked up to a gutter system around the roofs to collect rainwater. At the other end of the island he built a two-room house for his laundress, a woman named Mrs. Delancey, who would trudge the mile and a half to the other end and handwash all the laundry each day.

Finally he imported a zoo of monkeys, peacocks, turkeys, pheasants, parrots and iguanas to populate his paradise garden. For 14 years Salt Cay bloomed under the affectionate hands of Van Winkle, who came down for three months each winter, directing improvements and sharing his romantic monument with the public, whom he brought out every day on his yacht, the *Alice*, for $1 a head.

Atkinson puffed on his cigar, watching the increasingly somber couple across the table. He wanted the surprise to be total, and he wished he could be there to see their reaction. Breakfast was over and he had held them long enough; it was time to show them the *Alice*. They walked a couple of blocks through quaint pastel streets until they reached the yawl. John T.'s eyes widened when he saw it;

the 40-foot boat was even statelier than he imagined, her sleek hull freshly painted jet black, tall white masts piecing the sky. Three black sailors in spotless creased white uniforms waited to take them out to the island. Atkinson introduced them to the captain, a rare, pureblood Carib Indian named Alfred Sweeting, who had worked for Van Winkle. Sweeting helped the couple aboard and cast off while Atkinson, grinning broadly, waved from the shore.

The yawl slowly — glacially, it seemed to the newlyweds — motored east through the harbor, past wharves crowded with sloppy, colorful fishing smacks laden with conchs and sponges while their occupants shouted to each other in that peculiar singsong Caribbean patois. They slid past Fort Montague, its guns long silenced and now just a tourist attraction, until they rounded the east end of Hog (now Paradise) Island and went through the Narrows, a shallow channel between Hog and Athol Islands.

"Dare 'tis, Misser McCutcheon," said Captain Sweeting.

What they saw only confirmed their worst fears. Two miles away a long, thin band of mossbacked grey limestone rock stretched across the northern horizon, bleak and forbidding and not a beach in sight. There was a rough chop on the south side approach so Sweeting took the boat around the east end of the island to the calmer north side. John T. and Evelyn were awestruck as they got their real look at Salt Cay.

The beaches — fantastic gleaming white beaches — stretched nearly two miles down the coast, broken in places by 40-foot cliffs, rocky promontories, and piles of jagged boulders. Above the rich green vegetation, which spilled onto the sand, they could see the tops of hundreds of coconut palms dancing in the breeze. Atop one high cliff was the long, low red roof of the Main House that Van Winkle had restored, surrounded by more palms and casuarina trees. East of the cliff they could see two more red roofs, the guest cottages, nestled next to a beach in their own little grove. The crew dropped anchor in the turquoise water 50 yards out and sculled the couple ashore in a dinghy. A dozen black staff had assembled on the beach, anxious to meet the new owner.

"We followed an aisle of clipped casuarinas to the house," John T. wrote later, *"a low rambling bungalow with broad porches and cool airy rooms, the most suitable dwelling imaginable. There were cocoanut mats, wicker chairs, a faded rosewood sofa and a wide desk, a roll of charts, a telescope and a case a seafaring books. Shuttered doors, faded coppery green, were heavy to resist the battering of storms. The windows were salty from spray. Gloucester hammocks hung in sheltered corners. Two bedrooms adjoined the living room, with cedar closets, and beyond — an honest-to-gosh bathroom. The long veranda connecting the Main House with the service quarters was bordered with potted palms. A stone kitchen was immaculately whitewashed; a glowing wood stove was set back in the chimneybreast.*

"From the part of the porch where the dining table stood, an arbor covered with bougainvillea led down some steps to a stone path bordered with spider lilies and hibiscus, which soon branched three ways. We followed these paths as if in a trance. One led to the east, down a steep incline, past a sandy cove,

then on and on to a little crescent beach tucked between ridges of sharp weather-beaten rock. A hexagonal bathhouse, a sort of little pavilion, stood there, with steps to the roof, from whence the rising of the moon could be seen to spectacular advantage.

"The middle path led us below the overhanging cocoanuts until we emerged onto a stone pier extending out into the lagoon a couple of hundred yards across and a quarter mile long. Beside the pier were two stonewalled storage pools or crawls well stocked with brightly colored fish. On the opposite side of the lagoon a cut had been blasted through the limestone to the sea, twice a day the tide flowed in, transforming what had been a malodorous salt marsh into this clear lake. Beside the cut a high frame tower had been rendered somewhat perilous by lightening. At anchor in this peaceful haven lay the entire auxiliary fleet — a fishing smack, a dinghy, a skiff and a canoe.

"The third path led around to the west end of the lagoon, past the cottages of the caretaker and his assistant, to the Custom House, a thatched shelter surmounting a flight of stone steps, at the bottom of which a heavy drawbridge did duty as a pier. It could be lowered to receive the occupants of a boat, then raised to stand high and clear of the devastating rages that might otherwise wash it away."

That night, deliciously exhausted, the honeymooners sat down to their first meal on Salt Cay. Dinner was prepared by the staff and announced with the tinkling of a supper bell. During the negotiations the year before, Van Winkle's son, Todd, had written in a letter, "There is a great treasure on the cay and it is not buried, but there are many people who could not find it." Now John T. knew what he meant. Raising a glass of champagne in a toast with Evelyn, he said, "I rechristen thee Treasure Island." Above the table, on a wooden board hung from the ceiling and written in white script, was a stanza from a poem by William Cowper:

I am monarch of all I survey.
My right there is none to dispute;
From the center all around to the sea
I am lord of the fowl and the brute.

chapter two
the adventurer

The year was 1898. From where he sat on the bridge of the battleship John T. could clearly see the green-mounded islands that dotted the horizon off Luzon in the Philippines. He borrowed a pair of binoculars from the Officer of the Deck to study them more closely, then handed them back and slid down in his armchair, his feet resting on the railing. The officer had been with him during the Battle of Manila when John T. was one of only three correspondents present to cover the battle. Often this officer had been on the same ship and they had spent long hours trading stories and dreams. Both, it turned out, were fascinated with islands.

"Think you could live on one of those?" asked John T., pointing to the distant mounds.

"Dunno," said the officer, surveying the dense foliage covering the mounds. "Looks like you'd have to do a lot of chopping to clear away some land. But they sure look interesting, don't they?"

The battleship sliced through the calm sea while a seagull furiously tried to keep up, flapping and screeching through the clear Pacific sky. "You know," said John T. after a moment, "someday I'm going to own an island, a whole island all to myself. I'm not sure where I'm going to find one, especially on my salary, but I figure there's got to be one somewhere that's just right. And when I do I'll invite you down and we can do some chopping together."

The officer smiled. "When you do, let me know and I'll buy into it with you."

The ship passed close to a cluster of small islands. John T. pointed to the largest one. "I'll take that one, and that one and maybe that one there, just for good measure." They both laughed and lapsed into thoughtful silence. John T.'s mind wandered back to his boyhood days in Indiana, where he grew up a few miles south of Lafayette. In those days the territory had only recently been wrested from the Shawnee, and he used to listen intently to tales of Indian wars and pioneer struggles told by wrinkled old men from well-worn porch swings, stories still as fresh as the dying embers of a fire. Someday, he was convinced, he would taste similar danger and romance — just as soon as he could get out of Indiana.

He recalled an old mudflat on the Wabash, which surfaced only when the river was at its lowest. Until he first went abroad it was the closest thing to an island he'd ever seen, and he used to defend it with a fury born of a fertile imagination against murderous onslaughts from companion-turned-invaders. Once he and some friends uncovered a motherlode of what appeared to be gold underneath some rocks in a shady grove, hiding it with a obliging shopkeeper (who knew it was only mica) until they were distracted and went on to other things. When we went on to Purdue University (Class of '89) he purchased a cheap, decrepit skiff and named it the *Fanchon*. It remained moored on the riverbank — he never went out in it — yet he proudly pointed it out to his friends whenever he walked by until it disintegrated and washed downstream.

His first trip abroad was to Europe. At the time he was working for the Chicago Daily News, his first real job since moving to the city, when he and a colleague became possessed by a desire to do some traveling. They each saved up $500 over a year and boldly approached their editor, fully expecting to be fired when they told him their plans. Instead, the editor just stared at them and said, "That'll be a nice trip. Send home two illustrated stories a week and I'll keep on with your salaries." And that, thought John T. as the ship's bell signaled the change of shifts, was how easy it had been to become a foreign correspondent.

He got up, stretched, and wandered up to the bow. By tomorrow he'd be in Hong Kong and a few days after that in China, where he was supposed to file some stories for the Record. After that it was home — finally, after two and a half long years — but not before a side trip to check out the tail end of the Boer War in southern Africa.

John T. hadn't expected to be away this long. He had jumped at an invitation to accompany the U.S. Navy's new revenue cutter *McCulloch* on her maiden voyage, thinking he'd be at sea only a few months. There had been some debate among Navy officials in Washington where it should go. John T. over the years had acquired many influential friends in the Navy, who in turn benefited from the friendly press John T. provided. So when he asked them to redirect the *McCulloch* to a new route around the world they were receptive. It was still the age of Colonialism, and it wasn't difficult to convince the Navy that showing the flag in all these ports he wanted to see would also be good for the country.

Months later he and another colleague, Ed Harden of the New York World, found themselves in Colombo, Sri Lanka, trying to decide whether to stay with the *McCulloch* or take a French ship moored in the next berth to India, catching up with the *McCulloch* in Japan. It was a difficult decision so they flipped a coin. The coin said to stay with the *McCulloch*. The night after they left Colombo the French ship burned at the pier. A few weeks later they found themselves in the midst of the battle of Manila. A scowl clouded John T.'s face as he recalled the battle; he was still upset that Harden had beaten him to the world-wide scoop on the story because, unlike John T., he knew enough to put "Special Urgent" on his cable. No matter; he'd seen a lot of action, and as he headed to the officers' mess for dinner he was satisfied he was doing exactly what he'd always wanted to do.

His reporting has brought him a good deal of fame, both as a cartoonist and correspondent. In 1903 The Chicago Tribune lured him away from the Record. He remained with the Trib until his retirement forty years later, eventually winning a Pulitzer Prize and the label dean of American editorial cartoonists. As one of only a few cartoonists in the nation he was among the newspaper world's elite, friends with nationally known personalities. He was the Trib's prized possession whose popularity in the Chicago area helped boost the paper to new heights of circulation. He knew he was in demand and slyly extracted an unusual concession from the Trib: that he be allowed time off occasionally between contracts. The arrangement later allowed him to spend three months each winter on Treasure Island.

Too much time in Chicago grated on John T., and periodically he would find a way to satisfy his global wanderlust. On such occasions he would hire other cartoonists from around the country to substitute one cartoon a month while he was gone. In 1904 he took off for Japan, spent four days covering the Russo-Japanese War and was back at his desk 38 days later. In 1906 he and a friend made a five-month trek through central Asia, southeast of the Caspian Sea. They were mobbed in Iran, arrested in Turkestan and robbed in Russia. In Askhabad, Russia, they hired a carriage to take them to Meshed, Persia, (now Iran) a sacred city second only to Mecca among Moslems. From there they rode a horse caravan 250 miles through the central Asian wilderness to Osh, Russia, and on to Sinkiang, China, hitchhiking with more caravans and river steamers into Siberia and back to civilization via the Trans-Siberian Railway. They wanted, he said later, to get off the beaten tourist track.

In 1907 he returned to Europe with U.S. Senator Albert Beveridge and spent evenings in Paris with author Booth Tarkington, an old fraternity friend. Two years later he traveled to Kenya where he rode a hot air balloon and hunted big game with former President Teddy Roosevelt, who had just left office. One afternoon in Chicago a few months later, he happened to meet Orville Wright, who was busily trying to promote his new invention. John T. had always been fascinated with flight, and he got Wright's permission to fly along, perched on the lower wing of the fragile biplane for about fifteen minutes. His acquaintance with Wright enabled him to pull one of his most talked-about stunts a year later.

The occasion was Chicago's first Aviation Meet, held in Grant Park. A huge crowd was gathering to watch these newfangled contraptions that flew in the clouds above their heads. Backstage, John T. approached Wright to ask if he could fly as a passenger in one of his planes. Wright agreed, and the cartoonist returned to the bleachers, where he was sitting in the company of some lady friends. He said not a word about his plan.

John T. was at the time one of the city's most eligible bachelors, and he enjoyed that role immensely. He was that dashing adventurer whose tales of foreign intrigue and danger made for fascinating reading in the newspapers. He was an excellent storyteller and could hold a dinner party enthralled with graphic descriptions of Africa or Mexico's Pancho Villa.

The Aviation Meet provided an opportunity John T. couldn't resist. As he spied his plane being moved out onto the field, John T. removed his hat and turned to his companion. "Will you hold this for me, please? I'm going to fly in this race," he told her. Leaving his startled companion in her seat, he strode out onto the field, fastened himself in the plane and took off. His pilot was a man named Coffin, and two planes crashed that day, one just before and one during the race. The two pilots were, he recalled later, "the only ones killed in the meet." The ladies loved it.

But there was still the nagging matter of an island. In 1914 an acquaintance showed him a prospectus about an island for sale in Australia called Melville Island, located about 40 miles from Darwin on the northern frontier. The place was so large it showed up on maps of the globe, one and a half million acres of grass sagebrush and desert kept well manicured by a herd of 20,000 buffalo. The prospectus optimistically pointed out the herd's invest- ment potential: "The tongues are delicious and could be tinned, the tails will yield an excellent sample of tinned oxtail soup. Hoofs should be turned into glue and gelatin and bones into bone dust. Offal and meat fibers from the extract works into fertilizer..." And it all cost only £10,000.

In his office John T. read over the prospectus for the forth time. It wasn't precisely what he was looking for and Blackbeard had certainly never been there. But he was determined to buy an island, and he decided to go to Australia to check it out. At the time mutual hostility was developing between the United States and Mexico, and it looked like another war might break out. Mexico was in the general direction of Australia — south, anyway — so he got permission from the Navy Department to join the battleship *Wyoming*. He joined the ship in New York and informed the astonished captain of his orders to sail an hour before they were officially received.

At Vera Cruz John T. stayed with the U.S. fleet for several weeks, traveling inland to interview Pancho Villa and General Carranza. He returned to the ship from Villa's headquarters in Chihuahua, trying to decide what to do next. He still had three months of leave left from the paper, enough time for Melville Island. A steamer was leaving San Francisco in five days and he flipped another coin. The coin told him to stay with Carranza, who was about to make his triumphant march into Mexico City. Two days after the steamer left San Francisco the World War broke out in Europe, and John T. found himself heading in the opposite direction from Australia. For nearly two years he covered the Great War, dashing through the front lines to cover it from both sides and becoming one of the first correspondents to witness a battle from an airplane. He never did make it to Australia and when he returned to Chicago there was Atkinson, propping the advertisement about Salt Cay on his desk.

chapter three
island life

Punching bag, boxing gloves, movie camera and film, surfboards from Abercrombie and Fitch, Chinese lanterns, ash trays and fingerbowls from Japan, field glasses, hammocks, stationery embossed with the Treasure Island crest (a facetious seal John T. had dreamed up) sailor suits for Captain Sweeting and his men. Evelyn rattled off the list while her husband numbly stared at the boxes piled high in the garage of their large Lake Forest home. Their infant son, Jackie, lay swaddled in blankets at his feet, sleeping peacefully. They would pick up cases of tinned food in New York — enough to last everyone three months — but these items simply had to be purchased here because they wouldn't have much time in New York before the boat left for Miami. The shops in Nassau wouldn't have even heard of surfboards, much less sold them.

It was their third year as owners of Treasure Island, and they were gradually learning the vagaries of island life. Just getting there was proving to be a major expedition: two long days by train to New York, another couple of days by ship to Miami — where they often stayed overnight at Vizcaya, James Deering's palatial winter mansion — and finally by steamer to Nassau. John T. glanced down at his son — the first of three Evelyn eventually produced — and marveled at his ability to sleep through almost everything. Last year a destroyer had collided with their ship in a heavy fog just outside New York, ripping a fifty-foot gash right under their stateroom. Jackie hadn't even stirred. Fortunately the sea was glassy and their ship was able to limp back to New York, where the family caught another boat to Miami. But it was the closest call John T. would ever experience.

John T. watched the mountain of boxes being loaded onto the truck and again thanked heaven he had gone with Carranza that day and missed the boat to Melville Island. It would have taken a year just to get there and another one to get back. And he never did have much interest in buffalo. He reached into a side pocket and pulled out a stained, frayed letter, postmarked Nassau. It was from Cyril Solomon, their Man Friday in Nassau.

Without any of yours to reply to, the present serves to enclose account for November, which I trust you will find in order.

I am having the Alice *taken out of her shed to be repaired and repainted, and hope to get the new cylinders for her next week.*

The carpenter got through the odd jobs at the cay last Saturday, but up to now I cannot get one of them to fix the tower.

With nothing further to report, and my very kindest regards to yourself and Mrs. McCutcheon,

Cyril Solomon

John T. was glad that Solomon, who had been Van Winkle's agent, stayed on when he took over. A dignified white Bahamian, owner of a local tobacco and pipe shop,

Solomon handled all the day-to-day affairs of the island, paying the bills and wages for the two permanent caretakers, procuring supplies, hiring extra help for special jobs, escorting guests to the *Alice* for the ride to the island and transmitting cables, since the island had no electricity and direct communication with the Outside World was impossible.

Solomon had full authority and acted mostly on his own, leaving Evelyn and John T. little to do except send down an occasional check and just enjoy the place. Once Solomon noticed a large bill for guava jelly, which John T. dispensed in enormous quantities to voracious "banana" birds that fluttered about the breakfast table each morning. The next year there was a whole case of it in the pantry when the family arrived, thoughtfully purchased wholesale by Solomon from the guava factory on Harbour Island. Just before the winter season he would hire a cook, a laundress, a maid and a nurse for the child. Then he would cable Captain Sweeting at his ramshackle out-island farm with instructions to catch a boat to Nassau and fix up the *Alice*. John T. knew the island would be in perfect shape when he arrived, and that Solomon would be on the pier waiting to help transfer all those boxes.

Gradually routines were forming, hardening into traditions that would last for decades. Every morning promptly at 7 a.m. one of the caretakers would ring a ship's bell hung from a pole near the center of the island, signaling uniformed maids to deliver brass jugs full of steaming water to each of the bedrooms. "Yuh hot water, suh," the maids would whisper through shuttered doors, waking the occupants so they could shave in enamelware pans, empty them in the bushes outside, then go for a morning dip on the South Beach or play a quick game of shuffleboard on the tennis court next to the cottages before breakfast.

Breakfast was always served at the Main House under the south veranda on a round dining table made antproof by placing the Japanese fingerbowls filled with salt water under each leg. After the meal John T. would retire to his bedroom to draw the day's cartoon while the others gossiped or lounged around on hammocks until 10 a.m., when a creaking wheelbarrow loaded with a huge block of ice for the icebox announced the daily arrival of the *Alice* at the Custom House.

The Custom House was actually a small shelter on the island south side just west of the lagoon. From the shelter a set of concrete steps was carved down to the water's edge, where a large drawbridge had been erected that could be lowered out over the water. Guests and supplies were lowered into a dinghy and brought to the drawbridge. The yacht, which was permanently moored in Nassau — it was too large to get through the cut — brought out the mail, newspapers, supplies and any new guests to the Custom House, remaining offshore until around 4 p.m., when it returned to town with outgoing mail, the cartoon and the guests.

John T. looked at his watch and finished the last touches on his cartoon. It was 11 a.m., time for his daily swim. He put away his pens, donned a bathing suit and joined Evelyn and Charles Atkinson down at the Grotto, their favorite beach. Putting the watch beside him he laid on his stomach

place he knew where one could spend a profitable and perfectly delightful afternoon just counting the number of times a warbler attacked a mirror.

Life on Treasure Island acquired a pace entirely of its own. Time was calibrated to the languid gait of the shifting tides or approaching storms. The phrase, "Too late, but never mind," a line from a local folk song, was adopted for the island motto because it characterized so well the yawning, so-what attitude which ruled the island. If someone didn't get to do something he wanted, or some problem didn't get fixed right away, a chorus of voices would sing out, "Too late, but never mind!"

Since radio broadcasts had yet to reach the Bahamas and wireless transmitters were useless without electricity, news of the Outside World became far less important than knowing which way the wind was blowing, a fact that governed the day's activities. The essence of island living, after all, was total isolation from the rest of civilization, the ultimate counterpoint to the symphony of human activity, a little star in the terrestrial heaven.

If anyone came up with a serious or "northern" idea he was quickly ostracized from the Nobody Home Society, a humorous social device in which nobody responded to such unsettling comments. Years later someone brought down a radio, one of those huge wooden domed jobs with a large battery and a round, unblinking dial that seemed to perpetually stare at everyone. For a few days the islanders stared back at the contraption, listening in vaguely uncomfortable fascination to the Glenn Miller tunes it spewed out. Then John T. decided it interfered too much with the drone of the surf and gave the thing to one to the care-takers.

Watching new visitors gradually shift from fourth to first gear as they adjusted to this placid existence provided a good deal of amusement for John T. and Evelyn. Often he would recount the tale of the woman from New York who came down for a week one spring. Although a newspaper — usually the Tribune or the New York Times — was delivered daily with the *Alice*, nobody in good standing with the Nobody Home Society actually read them, except John T., who had to get new cartoon ideas.

This particular woman, however, was addicted to news-papers. On her first day she tore down to the Custom House when the boat arrived, snatched the paper from a sailor and buried her head in the newsprint for hours. The second day she elected to wait for the papers to be brought up to the house, whereupon she dove into a hammock with it for maybe an hour until it was time to hit the beach. On the third day she happened to be down beachcombing, glancing only at the headlines when she eventually came up for lunch. By the fourth day she was ignoring the news-papers altogether, and John T. would always conclude the story with the comment that she had come down with a particularly bad case of Island Fever.

chapter four
island projects

They were just lying half-buried in the muck at the bottom of Nassau harbor: two massive old fortress cannons that workmen repairing one of the town's forts obviously thought were worthless and had unceremoniously dumped in the water. John T. leaned over the edge of the *Alice* as it cruised into the glassy harbor to get a better look as they passed over the cannon. He enjoyed adding his own touches to what Van Winkle had created. Once he and his father-in-law, Howard Shaw, cleared away an area east of the lagoon and created an eight-tee golf course — eight tees, one hole. He didn't use it much (all his balls landed in the lagoon), but it was nice to look at until the native shrubbery wrested it away from him a few years later.

Then there was the second tennis court, which was supposed to replace the decaying old one next to the cottages. It was painted a bright green, and a chain link fence was constructed around the concrete slab. A few rounds of tennis were played on the court that season, but by the time they arrived the next year, the salt air had corroded the fence so much it was made useless. No one ever played tennis on it again.

Now as he looked at the cannons from the boat, he wondered if he could get them to the island somehow.

They were on their way to spend the night with publisher Frank Nelson Doubleday, who had a house east of town, and the Governor of the Bahamas was expected to be there. He decided to ask the governor's permission to haul them away. The governor had merely looked at him skeptically and laughed when John T. joked that he needed them for protection from pirates. The next year Howard Shaw organized an expedition and raised the cannons with block and tackle, dragging them on submerged wooden platforms the four miles to the lagoon, where they were left on the bottom to protect them from atmospheric corrosion.

The cannons lay there a couple of years while everyone tried to figure out what to do with them. Obviously a fort was needed — can't have a gun without a fort. So while John T. and Evelyn were off motoring by convertible automobile from Peking to the Trans-Siberian Railway through Mongolia's Gobi desert — John T. had gotten wanderlust again — his architect father-in-law constructed a small fort on the cliff next to the Main House. In a notch cut out of the wall he put one of the cannons on a specially built gun emplacement. Shaw christened the edifice Fort Canopus because he felt it was the best vantage point for looking at the star Canopus.

Whether it was actually the best place for viewing the star became the subject of a quite serious debate the next year. Some insisted they could see the star just as well from the South Beach, or better yet, the tip of the island. The argument was never really resolved so later, when John T. catalogued all the island songs in a small booklet, a footnote was inserted under a tune about Canopus, the star.

"Canopus is visible from all parts of the island. It is seen to advantage from the parapet of Fort Canopus, but the best view is from the tower, which is a half mile nearer the star," the notation said.

The fort was a solid work of masonry, which hung like a gigantic lead weight on the island's fragile limestone shoulder, a fact conveniently ignored in the whimsy of the moment. The oversight was realized decades later after World War II, when a slight crack appeared in the cliff behind the fort. Over the next several hours the crack widened. Sometime during the night the entire structure, cannon and all, collapsed with a loud crash at the bottom of the cliff. The end of the fort was termed a casualty of the war, when the island was requisitioned for a year by the Allies for use as a secret training base for three teams of British and American underwater demolition squads. Explosives and depth charges were blown up regularly around the island, and in the evenings, just for fun, they would toss hand grenades over the cliff. It was felt the concussions so weakened the cliff that it caused the fort to collapse.

There was still the problem of what to do with the other cannon, which was still lying on the lagoon bottom, now occupied intermittently by moray eels and lobsters. A solution presented itself one year when a massive hurricane hovered over the Bahamas for several days, rendering a rickety wooden tower built by Van Winkle next to the cut almost useless. After the storm the tower was shoved into the sea and Howard Shaw supervised construction of a new three-story tower with two-foot thick masonry walls, battlements and arched windows on top. The cannon was placed next to it, pointed out over the cut entrance in a menacing gesture towards Rose Island three miles away.

Of course, a monument such as this had to be formally dedicated. John T. and Evelyn sent out engraved invitations to everyone they could think of, including President Calvin Coolidge, whom they had met a couple of times. Coolidge, citing other pressing matters, wrote back that he couldn't make it, but the Governor, the Bahamian Speaker of Parliament, the American Consul and dozens of other dignitaries did. During the Governor's speech, a pirate in pantaloons and brandishing a cutlass lunged from the bushes into the crowd. John T. singlehandedly subdued him and shoved him into the tower, locking the door. A few minutes later the pirate appeared at the top of the tower, swinging by his neck at the end of a rope suspended from a gibbett. The matter concluded, the ceremony continued until Captain Sweeting, who was supposed to light some fireworks from the pier across the lagoon following the ceremony, decided to test one out. A loud explosion echoed over the island and the startled guests turned to see Sweeting tumbling from the pier into the water. The rest of the event was punctuated by more explosions, sparkling streamers and starbursts as Sweeting, transfixed, prematurely lit the rockets one after another like a child discovering a fascinating new toy.

During his years of traveling John T. collected rocks as souvenirs of each place he had visited. He had a brick from the Great Wall of China, a tile from Tamerlane's tomb in Samarkand, rocks from Napoleon's grave, a Ming Tomb,

Macchu Picchu, Jean Lafitte's blacksmith shop in New Orleans, stones from Marrakesh, Mt. Pelee, Karnak, a great Pyramid, the Acropolis, Bethlehem, Alhambra, the Seychelle Islands, Madagascar, the Galapagos, the Spice Islands, the Dutch East Indies, the Grand Canyon and Sri Lanka. He had a piece of Ft. Sumpter and another one from Ft. Johnson, which fired on Ft. Sumpter. He even had a rock from Bridgetown, Barbados, simply because George Washington once had smallpox there.

What John T. needed for all these rocks was a display case. So holes were chiseled out of the masonry on the tower's ground floor and the rocks were pasted into the wall with India ink labels scrawled below each stone identifying it. When that job was completed the tower was finished.

Except for one last item. Since the island was totally isolated from the Outside World — the only way to communicate was to take a boat in — John T. felt something had to be devised to contact help in an emergency. So he arranged with some Bahamians manning a quarantine station on Athol Island near Nassau to keep an eye on the tower. If they ever saw a sheet hanging from it during the day, or a lantern at night, that meant trouble and help was to be summoned. A year later two metal poles supporting metal-banded baskets were placed on top of the battlements. Coconuts could be burned in the baskets to signal for help. But in all the years the McCutcheon family owned Treasure Island, this low-tech system was never needed.

the social register

(ITEM) March 29, 1929 — Nassau, Bahamas (Chicago Daily News Service) — Richard T. Crane Jr. has the distinction of paying the first customs fee, an English penny, to John T. McCutcheon's new Custom House at Treasure Island. Richard E. Howe, the late James Deering's brother-in-law, Arthur Meeker and the Chauncey McCormicks were the next in line with the Duchess of Torlonia, having come down from Miami on the Seaborn, *and today the Acting Governor of Nassau, the Honorable C. Burns and Mrs. Burns followed suit. The Cranes came down on the yacht* Atlantic *which they chartered from the Vanderbilts and aboard were Mrs. Harlow Higgenbotham of Joliet and Mrs. Joseph Medill Paterson.*

Vice President of the United States and Mrs. Charles Gates Dawes, who are due in Miami Beach next Saturday to be the guests of Mr. and Mrs. Isaac C. Elston, Jr., formerly of Chicago, in their oceanfront home, will pass the weekend with the McCutcheon's. At any rate, the Vice President will do so, but as Mrs. Dawes is not the best sailor in the world she may remain with the Elstons while Gen. Dawes comes down to Nassau....

It was time for another chowder party. John T. quickly counted the number of guests as they came up the steps from the Custom House drawbridge and whispered to one of the men, who sprinted off down the path to warn the cook how many people to expect. One never knew who was coming until they actually arrived. Sometimes invited guests sent last-minute regrets with Captain Sweeting, but other times they were simply left stranded in Nassau when Sweeting, who never could keep track of time very well, left ahead of schedule. Too late, but never mind. This group was dressed in the custom of the day, the men in light seersucker suits and the ladies corseted in long-sleeve, ankle-length dresses and topped with wide-brimmed, flowered hats. John T. remembered the time the Duke of Kent had wandered about the island in a loose shirt and baggy shorts while he, the King of Treasure Island, was always dressed impeccably. He glanced down at his new pair of sneakers, already coming apart, and noted how fast they disintegrated.

Among certain social circles in Chicago and elsewhere it was becoming a mark of distinction to be invited to McCutcheon's private island. But John T. could never quite get over the fact that he, once a poor farm boy, was now hosting numerous European Earls, Counts, Dukes and Duchesses. They were joined by American luminaries of the period such as Drew Pearson, authors John Dos Passos, James Thurber, Arthur Crock, Archibald MacLeish and Kenneth Roberts. Many of the Americans were his friends; others, such as Roberts, were trespassers who just appeared, while most of the Europeans were guests of the current Governor. All the Governors (the British Foreign Office transferred them frequently) had standing invitations to visit the island whenever they wished.

One afternoon Crown Prince Paul of Greece came over, the guest of the then-Governor. Evelyn's sister, Theo, was assigned the task of entertaining the Prince. She showed him around the island and demonstrated how two people could lie foot-to-foot on the huge hammock in the chowder grove next to the lagoon. The soon-to-be-king fell asleep in the hammock and Theo, afraid to wake him, had lain motionless for two full hours until the Prince awoke.

Years later the British government appointed Edward, Duke of Windsor, as Governor. He and the Duchess would drop by occasionally and sip whiskey sours and eat de-onionized chowder (in deference to the Duchess, who hated onions) on the north porch. On one of their first visits the Windsors were invited to go swimming with the group. They were shown John T.'s bedroom, a modest room with two single beds and a couple of bureaus in the Main House, where they were to change their clothes. Presently Evelyn heard giggling through the thin walls; the giggling grew more intense until the pair emerged properly dressed for bathing. Evelyn was later told the Windsors had never seen each other undress before.

In later years author John Marquand became the island's first regular renter. Charles Lindbergh and his wife, Anne, who were friends of the Marquands, came down once for a two-week visit while John T. and Evelyn were also there. The Lindberghs lived down at the South Beach bath-house and refused to talk with Evelyn after she tried to shoot a photograph of the reclusive flyer. They remained in the South Beach cottage and came up to socialize only for meals. Anne Morrow Lindbergh wrote part of her book,

"Gift From The Sea," during her stay on Treasure Island.

Reporters sometimes shadowed visiting socialites, returning stateside later to write up breathless accounts of the place, which of course heightened the island's fame still further. Typical was the account of Katrina McCormick, a journalist with a newspaper in downstate Illinois.

KATRINA DROPS DOWN TO NASSAU; VISITS FAMOUS TREASURE ISLAND
OUR GOTHAM REPORTER
TAKES A FEW DAYS OFF AND BASKS IN THE SUN
IN JOHN T. MCCUTCHEON'S ISLAND PARADISE

This sentence is called, in newspaper lingo, the lead. It should be made to catch your eye. The rest of the first paragraph follows the lead. Once that violent mental struggle is over the article is just as good as written. Let's skip it today. I've just come home from the Southland. I find my typewriter just as good as ever, but my fingers are rusty, not to mention my head.

(The next few paragraphs describe the reporter's arduous trip to Miami and Nassau, finally arriving at the pier where the island yacht is moored.)

"The Windrift *met us at the dock. Captain Sweeting said, "Mr. and Mrs. McCutcheon are waiting on the island for you." An hour in the boat took us to Treasure Island belonging to John T. McCutcheon, famous cartoonist of the Chicago Tribune. The McCutcheons were waving to us as we neared the island shore. In a few minutes we were splashing in the surf and*

basking in the sun...

"There has been criticism of late about the endings of news-paper stories. It is said that they peter out, the reader seldom finishes a column and never returns to the page where the article is continued. Let's skip that, too. I'm still on Treasure Island. Please give me one more week to get home."

Whenever guests arrived it was an Occasion, and a chowder party — the centerpiece of which was an elabo-rately prepared conch or grouper chowder — was called for. John T. would lead the newcomers the half-mile from the Custom House to the Main House, where Evelyn would be waiting to greet them. Forewarned, she would have instructed one of the caretakers to kill a large grouper from the fish crawl, and the cook would be in the kitchen busily preparing the afternoon meal. Meanwhile other maids would have prepared the grove, placing long, colorful tablecloths John T. had purchased in Madagascar over picnic tables. Place settings would be prepared and long benches lined up next to the tables, there not being enough chairs to go around.

Prior to lunch everyone would go for a swim, after which they would come up to the house for some pre-meal cock-tails, usually a fruity rum drink John T. enjoyed mixing. Around 2 p.m., a maid would come out and whisper to Evelyn, who would announce lunch was ready and every-one would traipse down to the grove, drinks in hand. Towards the end of the meal a caretaker would come down in a white uniform and sit down next to a palm tree, ser-enading the guests on his guitar with old Nassau songs while the canopy of palm trees whispered above, the glasses clinked and conversations continued in hushed tones.

Afterwards Evelyn would arise and announce a walk down the North beach to the caves. The cave was actually a large rock a mile and a half towards the western extremity of the North Beach. The larger of the two caves faced east and was deep enough to pitch a campsite out of the rain. The other, smaller cave, could be reached only by climbing down the eroded, razor-sharp northerly face. But it was a deep, well-protected cave that had a very unusual feature: a small hole in the ceiling through which one could stick his arm. A wiggling hand that looked as if it had sprouted from the limestone itself would startle unsuspecting guests standing atop the rock.

Those not wishing to digest their meal in that way could find a hammock — there were numerous ones scattered all over the island — until they returned. After the stroll the guests would all sign the register (which was becoming a rather valuable item) and head back to the Custom House and waved off the island by their tired but gracious hosts. The entire routine never varied and became one of the island's most longstanding traditions.

After the visitors had gone, John T. and Evelyn would go back to the Main House for a quiet, relaxed supper while the men raised the heavy drawbridge with huge hawser pulleys and sealed Treasure Island, once again from the Outside World behind a vast moat of azure water.

John T. McCutcheon. Adventurer, foreign correspondent, dean of American political cartoonists. His yearning to own a private tropical island led him to buy Salt Cay sight unseen for $17,500 in 1916. It came with a 40-foot yawl, a staff of twelve, a half dozen buildings and miles of beaches.

King Paul of Greece (standing), with Evan Morgan, Lord Tredegar, a direct descendant of the pirate Henry Morgan, on the North Beach.

The Duke and Duchess of Windsor, occasional guests on the island while the Duke was Governor of the Bahamas in the 1940s.

Charles T. Atkinson, the friend of John T.'s who found a small advertisement listing Salt Cay for sale and gave it to the cartoonist to think about.

The island's first ferry, the Alice, seen from the Custom House on the south side. The Custom House was for decades the main entrance onto the island.

The Custom House drawbridge was lowered each day when the island ferry anchored offshore. Dinghies took people and supplies between the drawbridge and the boat.

Fort Canopus, a concrete fort meant to frame an ancient fortress gun salvaged from Nassau harbor, on the cliff next to the Main House. The fort eventually fell into the sea.

The guest cottages just east of the Main House. These one-room bungalows, which still exist today, housed most of the guests who visited the island. A cistern between the two provided fresh water via hand pump. Kerosene lamps provided light.

The lagoon seen from the tower, looking north, circa 1922. All the coconut palms in this photo were planted.

The lagoon pier, around the same time. When boats could get through the cut, the lagoon pier became the entry point to the island.

The crawls next to the pier, in which were kept live trap-caught fish awaiting their turn in the kitchen.

The staff of the island in the mid-1920s, including cooks, a laundress, a caretaker, captain and crew.

A typical cluster of guests around the same time. Visitors included society queens, literati, European nobility, national politicians, even ordinary people.

The island was a child's paradise, with beaches, real forts and hammocks to play in. Here two family members cavort on the North Beach.

John T. with his son, Barr, at the Custom House. As the Owner, John T. always wore a hat and tie on the island.

My father clings to a boat's mast in the lagoon. Tutors were brought down on occasion, but education was a distant second to fun.

John T. (with the hat) on the North Beach, after the Great Hurricane.

Left, the first tower, a wooden affair that fell into the sea after a storm.

Right, the Alice, which decayed in the lagoon after losing its mast.

This Hong Kong ricksha was just narrow enough for the island paths. Other than by foot, it was the island's only means of transport.

The Main House living room, including the North Corner, the coziest spot on the island. The tabletop at right was a single piece of Philippine mahogany.

The Main House dining room, located on the south veranda next to the main entrance on the left. The round table could only seat eight comfortably.

chapter six
the umbilicus

They heard it before they saw it, a distant drone of engines that grew louder and louder until, in a deafening roar, the seaplane flew right over the Main House nearly at tree-top level. John T. and Evelyn rushed out to the cliff to see the plane make a wide banking turn and come back towards the island. Seaplanes had been around a few years, but except for the commercial craft that flew daily between Miami and Nassau, they were rare. This one, it was becoming clear, was going to land outside the cut.

They returned to the breakfast table to finish their morning coffee. Fifteen minutes later a dazed and soaking wet Captain Sweeting walked up the path, tears stream-ing down his face. My mother's died, thought John T.; or maybe our house in Lake Forest has burned down? He waited anxiously for Sweeting to explain.

"Boss," the captain began, taking off his dripping cap and staring at the ground, "I wuz drivin' up Bay Street in de hack wid de mail an' de hice. Jus' as I come insight, I hear de noise of de 'splosion an' I see Roy fly hup in de hair. Boss, I done hop out o' dat cab and run! I grab a hax layin' by a woodpile an' I jump right in de sea to scuttle her. But, boss, hit wuz too deep! Dey had to fetch me hout. Den dis gemman come alongside in his hairplane and hax me if I want to let y'all know."

"Know what?" asked John T.

"De *Lucaya*," she done burn hup!" The *Lucaya* was the new island yacht, purchased after the *Alice* was retired when a shed containing the boat's mast and rigging burned to the ground. The *Alice* was now resting on a sandspit in the lagoon, slowly decaying and soon to be used for firewood.

John T. took a deep breath and relaxed; it could have been something far worse. He looked at his captain again, fascinated that this loyal but unsophisticated employee had the guts to ride a seaplane out to tell him the news. No one had been injured, fortunately, and he could just instruct Solomon to buy another boat. "You've never flown before, have you," he asked Sweeting.

"Nossah, boss. I bin too scared to go hup. I hain't never wanted to try."

"Were you frightened now?"

"Well suh, boss. I bin so hupset 'bout de *Lucaya* I dint rightly know how I come over here. All I wanted wuz to get hout here quick's I kin."

John T. smiled, trying to make Sweeting feel a little better, and thanked him for making such an effort to tell him the news. He was quickly learning that boats — the essential umbilicus connecting the island with civilization — were one of the major headaches of owning an island. The *Lucaya*, he later learned, had blown up when one of the sailors lit a match to see how much fuel was in the tank.

Normally a knowledge of boats would be an essential tool for running an island, but John T. remained the complete landlubber. He knew next to nothing about them and couldn't tell the difference between a mast and a boom. For him repairing an engine or examining a new yacht was about as simple as a child trying to check out an airplane. As long as he could delegate such chores to someone else he was content. Obviously the *Lucaya* had to be replaced. In the meantime they would use the care-taker's small Bahamian sloop, not the most luxurious craft in the world.

A month or so following his return to Lake Forest a friend mentioned he'd seen a suitable auxiliary yawl for sale in Jacksonville, Florida, called the *Ocean Queen*. From his description it seemed exactly what John T. was looking for, so he negotiated its purchase by mail, the way he did with the island itself, which had proved so successful. That completed he and Evelyn left on another trip, this time through South America, flying over the Andes in rattletrap seaplanes (he found out later the plane he flew in crashed two weeks afterwards, killing everyone aboard), and cruis-ing down the Amazon. They were on their way back to the states aboard a freighter loaded with highly explosive brazil nuts when he received a cable from Jacksonville. It seemed the *Ocean Queen*, which was supposed to have been taken to Nassau, never made it. Instead, the brand-new yacht had foundered on some beach near Fort Pierce.

The captain who was supposed to sail her, a certain John Hanna, had hired a couple of sailors who turned out to be afraid of the sea. He himself preferred power over sail. Just outside Fort Pierce a storm blew up during the night. The engine began acting up, conking out more and more frequently, forcing Hanna to spend all his time below to keep it going. He left the helm to Olaf, one of the sailors, specifically instructing him to steer southeast so as not to get pushed too far towards shore.

Olaf, however didn't want to get out of sight of land and hugged the shoreline, finally heading for shelter toward three lights he thought were the marker buoys at the entrance to Fort Piece's channel. The lights, however, were three hotels and soon he had run the yacht into the surf, where it lodged on a sandbar. Olaf and the other sailor jumped ship but Olaf turned up the next day to help Hanna and the U.S Coast Guard in an unsuccessful attempt to free *Ocean Queen*. Then Olaf went berserk and had to be led away by the local sheriff. Hanna sat on the beach watching John T.'s yacht slowly sink in the sand, a total loss.

John T. had better luck a couple of months later when, again upon the recommendation of a friend, he purchased the *Windrift* (by mail, of course). It was a good 38-foot auxiliary yawl similar to the *Alice*. The *Windrift* served the island well for the next twenty years. It, too, eventually fell apart, but by then John T. had long since learned that he and boats just didn't get along well together.

Decades later, long after John T's death, the family purchased a wooden Bahamian sloop and named her *Lucaya II*. On a lazy, sunny afternoon in 1963 Evelyn, her nephew David King and the caretaker took it down to the far end of the island. About halfway down the engine caught on fire and the interior was quickly engulfed in flames. The three boarded a dinghy they were towing behind and watched in dismay as the sloop's twin 20-gallon gas tanks exploded, sending the deck in splinters as high as the mast. The hull was scuttled but it was, again, a total loss. No one ever named another island boat *Lucaya* again.

sammy

Sammy's eyes bulged in total panic. He had just got his first look at the *Lucaya* which was burdened under an incredible load, the water lapping almost to the gunwales. That morning he had asked John T. if he could bring a few friends over for a little party. Not many, ten or fifteen. Sammy was proud of his job as head caretaker; working on McCutcheon's island was a prestige position in those days and sometimes he liked to show off the place to his buddies in Nassau. He didn't think John T. would mind, and of course he hadn't.

But he didn't figure on this. When the *Lucaya* went back to town that afternoon, Sammy had gone with it to invite his friends over. Within an hour the word had spread up and down the waterfront that good ol' Sammy was throwing a party, and now there were hundreds of gaily-dressed, jabbering Bahamians all wanting in on the act. Sammy pushed his way through the crowd to get a better look at the boat. A group of oversized, straw-hatted women were perched on the boom, another two dozen or so were crammed below, more were stuffed around on the deck and a brass band was blaring out a new tune on the bow. He tried to cajole a few of them into getting off, but nobody budged.

Lordy, he thought, what if the boat sinks and all these people drown? He was absolutely positive their ghosts would hound him forever and the sweat streamed from his forehead in new gushes of fear. If that happened he'd have to get another jibdog, he was sure of that. He liked the one he had, but obviously it wouldn't be able to handle all those ghosts at once. The jibdog, or bitch dog, he once explained to John T., was better than the male because the male's hair stood on end whenever it met a ghost, rendering it powerless, while the jibdog's hair remained flat, keeping the ghost at bay until he could take certain measures, which he would never specify.

Sammy threw up his hands in despair, uttered a quick prayer and told Sweeting to cast off. There were 126 people on the 38-foot yawl. Luckily the sea was calm and Sweeting was still able to steer the craft, although he had to stand up and arch one leg over a woman's shoulder to reach the tiller with his toes. At the Custom House the drawbridge was ready, and two amazed caretakers watched from the top of the steps as the crowd gradually emptied onto the island. One woman fell into the sea but she was hauled out quickly, laughing and muttering. When everyone was ready Sammy signaled the group to start the walk to the old tennis court near the cottages where the party was to be held, the band cutting loose at the head of the procession.

Up at the Main House John T. and Evelyn waited, listening to the music grow louder and louder. Presently the band passed on the path before the house, followed in single file by partygoers, and more partygoers, and more and more people, followed at last by a subdued and apologetic

Sammy who tried to explain what had happened. Astonished but curious, John T. and Evelyn picked up a couple of wicker chairs and decided to join the party. Hurricane lanterns and globular Japanese candle lamps had been placed all around and in the trees at the tennis court, lending an eery but spectacular aura as the shadowy revelers danced and jigged to the music under a bright full moon. John T. and Evelyn sat at the edge of the court and every so often Sammy would bring friends up to be introduced, like courtier at an imperial gathering.

Finally, just before midnight, the last of the lamps flickered out, the band stopped playing and the tired crowd trudged back to the *Lucaya*. Carefully, they all boarded the boat and Sweeting headed back to Nassau while the band half-heartedly tried out another song. Sammy went back to report to John T., who was more than a little nervous about the status of his boat. "Boss, de las' time I see her, she wuz still afloat," said Sammy. But it wasn't until the next morning when the yawl rounded into sight around the end of Hog Island that they learned it had survived.

"Well, Sammy, I hope you'll be ready to sing for us tomorrow," John T. said later.

"Boss, I goin' to sing a verrry special service tomorrow. De Lawd he need some especial thanks for allowin' everybody to survive dis night!"

The Sunday sings had become another tradition, replacing the regular church services the staff wasn't allowed to attend in town during the season. Following supper all the staff would file out of the kitchen and sit in a semi-circle at one end of the darkened porch. John T.,

Evelyn and the guests sat at the other end. Sammy, and later Josephas Munroe, who took over as head caretaker years later, would get out his guitar and lead the two groups in singing simple, rhythmic Bahamian spirituals. The conclusion of the service was always signaled with the "Goodnight Song," in which each guest on the island was named in a particular verse.

During the 1960s the tradition began to die out, partly because the practice was too closely reminiscent of the antebellum South and reminded some of the younger family members that the pleasure of Treasure Island was made possible largely through the servitude of another race.

In fact, the lines dividing the two societies on the island were as sharp and well-defined as any southern plantation. Except for the maids who brought the hot water every morning, none of the staff — during the season there were seven or eight salaried employees, not counting the sailors — was allowed east of the Main House, where the guests slept, before breakfast. Similarly, none of the whites ever entered the kitchen area or the staff quarters. Social life for the maids and caretakers centered around Sammy's red-roofed shotgun house down the path west of the Main House, and the Sunday sings were the only regular activity the two groups engaged in together. The staff accepted and were comfortable with these rules, and this general attitude was never more apparent than in the case of Ronald Davis.

Ronald was one of those odd additions to island life that simply happened. One day he just appeared. No one had hired him, but he wanted to do something useful, so Levy Glass, a teetotaling martinet who succeeded Sammy when the latter took to the bottle, ordered him to be the official island fisherman. Every morning Ronald would head out in one of the dinghies with some hand lines and a long harpoon and catch fish and conch to keep the crawls well stocked. After a couple of years John T. put him on the payroll. Then he also became the official coolie, ferrying around guests on a rickshaw John T. had purchased in Hong Kong.

One year Ronald failed to appear as the staff gathered for the season. It turned out that during the preceding summer he had worked up a frothy rage against a woman in town and stabbed her, fortunately not fatally. He was arrested and sent to jail for a year. The following season he was released and soon was back on the island, fishing and hauling people around on the rickshaw. John T. put him on the payroll again without a second thought; after all, he was an excellent fisherman and the best damn coolie in the Bahamas. If someone had brought up the obvious, that Ronald might also be capable of stabbing a white woman, it would quickly have been dismissed as unthinkable. Furthermore, Ronald himself would have agreed.

chapter eight
buried treasure

R ight away they found the tree, a tall, crooked palm with gaping holes drilled into the trunk by foraging termites, just as Sammy had described. That morning he had come up to John T. and whispered urgently that he needed to talk to him privately. It seemed his wife Josephine, who was the island cook, had a terrible nightmare about buried treasure. In the dream she saw this tall palm tree with gaping holes in the trunk, and under the tree were some rotting boards, and under those was an iron chest full of treasure. She woke up in a cold sweat and had remained awake all night shivering under the covers.

All his life John T. had wanted to find buried treasure, although he knew his chances were slim at best. When he purchased the island he thought seriously for a while that such a treasure might exist somewhere on the place, but soon discarded the idea as a pipe dream. For a pirate, after all, burying treasure on Salt Cay was akin to stashing loot in Grand Central Station. Numerous pirates had indeed trafficked the place, but only to forage for salt from the marsh or to prepare to enter Nassau harbor only a few miles away. Instead, the notion became another harmless diversion, a topic for dinner table discussion and something to do whenever one was tired of reading, sleeping, swimming, sailing or surfing. John T. and his friends occasionally spent afternoons trying to think of the likeliest burying spots, then dug gopher holes all over the place, always, of course, without success.

This time he listened intently to Sammy's tale and then dashed off to the breakfast table to tell the group what he had planned for the morning's activities. After an hour or so of searching they found the tree. He and Charles Atkinson — Charles always seemed to be on hand at times like these — started digging though a thatch of matted casuarinas pine needles and dead palm branches until the astonished diggers came upon some rotting boards just as Josephine had predicted. They renewed their digging, the pile of sand getting higher as they deepened the pit. But all they found was just more sand and John T. finally gave up, mildly disgusted at another dry hole.

One afternoon a stranger appeared on the island lugging an odd-looking pole with a metal disk at one end connected to a big box with some dials on it. He had written John T. asking quite seriously if he could search for buried treasure on the island. Naturally, John T. agreed. The contraption, explained the stranger, was a metal detector and he intended to thoroughly comb the island with what he insisted was a foolproof device. For days the man wandered about, swinging the pole over the ground. He picked up a lot of rusty nails, some old chains and metal plates, but no treasure. After a week he gave up, convinced there was nothing on the island.

Later a guest happened to casually remark while the islanders were watching the sunset from the cliff that there was gold suspended in the ocean, some $30,000,000 of it in each cubic mile. The only problem was to extract it. A few days later the guest appeared with two wire fish traps stuffed with charcoal. The guest explained that, based on a complicated scientific formula he had spent hour in a hammock working on, the gold would precipitate onto the charcoal and the only real work would be to pull up the traps every so often and scrape off the metal. All he needed was a good place where a lot of water passed through. The cut seemed a perfect spot and John T. made some quick calculations: The tide flowed in and out four times every twenty-four hours; if they worked only five cubic miles of water each season, it would mean a cool $150,000,000 annually! But, like so many other things that never panned out, the project was mothballed, the traps were never set and Treasure Islanders were soon distracted by more feasible projects, like reading and sleeping and sailing and swimming.

Once John T. did dig up some buried treasure, although he had earlier planted it himself. The occasion was a Pirate Picnic given for some local charities, and the Governor had asked him to oversee a treasure hunt. Two boxes, painted to look like the real thing, were buried on what was then called Hog Island (since renamed Paradise), one containing a single twenty-dollar gold piece, the other a bag full of pennies. Then he drew up a map with "X"s marking the spots and handed copies out to all the participants. All afternoon people dug, but only the box with the gold piece was found.

The next day he and a companion went over to Hog

to retrieve the other box, but a young couple was lying right on the spot where it was buried. As the pair started digging nearby the couple became annoyed.

"What are you doing?" he demanded.

John T. stopped digging and mopped his brow. "We're digging for buried treasure," he said matter-of-factly.

The beachgoer stared at him blankly. "Right," he said. Well, I wish you'd dig somewhere else. This is our spot and you're bothering us."

"I apologize if we're troubling you," John T. said. "But we're pretty sure we're close to the right spot." He paused for effect. "In fact, would you be so kind as to move over a few feet? We believe the buried treasure is right under your picnic basket."

Muttering to himself, the man stood up. He wanted to protest, but his girlfriend didn't want a confrontation. She gathered their items and the couple moved a few yards down the beach, shaking their heads in disgust.

"Thank you very much," said John T. as he resumed digging where the pair had lain. Presently his shovel struck something hard and hollow. John T. and his friend got down on hands and knees and laboriously lifted a heavy box from the hole. They opened the lid and pulled out a large bag of coins. John T. tipped his hat, thanked the astonished couple for moving, and the pair staggered off down the beach with their load.

a family island

Evelyn needed a tutor. Her three boys — by then two more sons, Shawie and Barr, had arrived — were somewhere around on the island but she was darned if she knew where. That morning she had uncovered their grammar and arithmetic books from under a pile of comics and wet, salty towels. She had ordered them to complete chapters four and five before they headed off to play. But the texts still lay on the carved Philippine mahogany table in the living room where she had put them. She went out to the cliff and peered through binoculars at the north beach a mile away. They were there, all right, body surfing under the watchful eye of one of the caretakers.

Evelyn smiled and shook her head as she lowered the binoculars. It was understandable; Treasure Island was a children's paradise, complete with very real fortresses, ships, moats and drawbridges. Obviously the lure of this magnificent sandbox was infinitely more powerful than the repulsive discipline required to learn multiplication tables. She returned to the house to ask John T., who was busy sketching out another cartoon in the bedroom, what he thought about bringing a tutor down to educate the boys. Three months away from school each year was simply too long. She had heard of a good tutor in Chicago named

Arthur Abbott who had taught the children of some of her Lake Forest friends, and when John T. agreed it was a good idea she decided to call him when she got back to Chicago in April.

Abbott was fresh out of college and trying to make it as a free-lance teacher in Chicago, living with a pet cat in a rundown, sparsely-furnished two-room apartment in north Chicago. The residual odor of stale cigar smoke blended with smells from a well-used cat pan and the permanently unmade bed, which briefly dissipated whenever he opened the dusty, smudged windows. Besides the bed, he possessed a frayed, stuffed rocking chair, a rickety table with two equally-rickety chairs, a bookcase full of texts and adventure novels, and a small, cluttered dresser. Above the dresser were photographs of Tahiti, London, Paris and Istanbul, which he had cut out of travel brochures. The remains of the brochures, crumpled and well-fingered, were stuffed into the crowded drawer of his bedside table. Whenever he felt depressed he would pull out the brochures, look at the photographs, and dream that someday he would have enough money to see those places.

Thus he was predictably elated when Evelyn McCutcheon called him one afternoon with an amazing offer: a salaried, expense-paid three-month trip to this famous private island in the Bahamas he had read about in the local newspapers. This was his big chance to experience some of the exotica and adventure he had spent so much time reading and dreaming about in novels and travel brochures. Abbott was determined to have some fun on Treasure Island. As for the tutoring — well, that was a small price to pay.

He came down the following January with the rest of the family. One of the first things Evelyn did was sit him down and explain the island rules. With no electricity, everything was run with kerosene or wood and fire was a constant worry. Fresh water was precious and Evelyn had plastered notices above all the toilets asking they be flushed only on "major occasions." She had also put a list of rules on one of the green hurricane doors to the living room:

"NOBODY is allowed in the sea alone....TERRIBLE PENALTY for not anchoring or mooring the boats fast....TER-RIBLE PENALTY for roughhousing in the room with a lamp...SLIGHTLY LESS TERRIBLE PENALTY for mis-laying things...NO LITTER BUGS ALLOWED...It will be appreciated by the management if the living room and porches can be left reasonably neat and uncluttered at bedtime..."

Every morning after breakfast Abbott would herd the boys down to the Portable, the rigid screen and canvas tent John T. brought back from an African safari, and dutifully guide them through their studies for two hours. At 11 a.m. he would signal the end of the session, and the rest of the day his playful young charges would teach him all the secrets of the island. They showed him the art of sculling the heavy wooden dinghies around the lagoon, demon-strated the best spots for bodysurfing, took him sailing in the *Windrift* and guided him on long expeditions down the island's narrow backbone to the far end. He learned the best shell beaches and collected a motley bunch, which he carefully laid out on his bedroom bureau, critically examining each one like a jeweler checking out diamonds. Abbott was having the time of his life.

One afternoon the four of them walked all the way to the other end of the island, to the point where the bare limestone outcroppings gradually dwindled into the sea. It was a hot day and Abbott exuberantly got the urge to dive into the sea to cool off. Shawie warned him to watch out for the scabrous limestone spikes, which lined the edge of the island, and they watched skeptically while he arched out fully clothed over the edge into the water. When he surfaced blood was streaming down his face from a massive wound on his forehead, spreading out in the water around him. Abbott had hit the bottom. Laboriously, the boys lifted their stunned tutor back onto the island and splashed water from a stagnant pool filled with decaying seaweed onto his face, hoping the iodine they heard was produced in such pools would stop the bleeding. It took four long hours to walk him back to the Main House. Every so often he would faint from the wound, and by the time they got him back it was dark. John T. took one look and decided Abbott would have to go to the hospital in Nassau. The *Windrift*, however, had left for the day so he placed Abbott into the caretaker's small sailboat and headed for town through storm-tossed seas in total darkness. The poor tutor remained in the hospital for several days and finally left for Chicago to complete his recovery. He never returned to the island and Evelyn never hired another tutor.

The years passed. When they were old enough the boys were sent off to a boarding school near Boston, coming down to the island only on their vacations. Usually they brought down some friends, and for a few weeks each Spring the island would revert to a playground of puerile activity.

Then came World War II and the island became a training ground for special operations frogmen. Every day the trainees would swim seven miles around the island and practice demolition maneuvers on and around the place.

The following year John T. and Evelyn returned to inspect the damage the frogmen had done. It wasn't much: some broken chairs, bullet holes in the old palm tree at the head of the cliff (which didn't really damage it since woodpeckers looking for termites had already drilled thousands of holes in the trunk). There was a cracked cistern down at Delanceytown, Van Winkle's laundress' house, created when an inebriated soldier tossed a hand grenade in it. Nobody suspected at the time that the explosions had also loosened the cliff.

But Nassau had changed. During the war the Bahamian government had limited laborers' daily wages to four shillings a day. Many Bahamians went to the United States to help in the war effort and returned telling stories of much higher wages there. American contractors in Nassau, hired to construct a new airfield and other wartime facilities, agreed that Bahamian wages were too low. The resentment built up until in June, 1942, workers in Nassau rioted, leaving five people dead and Bay Street in a shambles. In response the Bahamian government lifted the daily wage to five shillings and the laborers, satisfied for the moment, returned to work. But a seed had been sown which would grow over the next three decades, and as the wage-price spiral continued to climb, it became more and more difficult for the McCutcheon family to sustain the island. The Bahamas had finally joined the rest of the world, with fatal consequences to Treasure Island.

When the war ended John T. was 73 years old and very frail. Evelyn took over an increasing share of the chores of running the place. She had always handled the day-to-day affairs during the season, but now she took on the added burden of issuing monthly instructions to Gurth Duncombe, who succeeded the retiring Solomon, and later Colin Honess, who took over as agent in 1963. John T., more and more arthritic, took to riding the rickshaw to get around. The rest of the time he would lie on a hammock and read or draw his one cartoon a week for the Tribune. When guests came over for chowder parties he remained up at the Main House, eating alone and waiting for the visitors to come up and offer the obligatory greeting.

In May, 1949, a month after he left the island, John T. died abruptly of a heart attack. The day he left Treasure Island for good was calm and clear. Josephas Munroe, who succeeded Levi as head caretaker just before the war, brought the *Guanahani*, a small Bahama sloop John T. had bought for emergencies, over to the pier and placed the old man in it so he could sit facing the stern, away from the sun's glare. He seemed to know he wouldn't be back and a feeling of deep gloom settled over the staff as he said goodbye to each one. On the way into town Josephas and Wilfred Sweeting — Wilfred had taken over from his uncle as captain — sang some old island songs while John T. watched the island receding in the distance.

chapter ten
a new generation

I was only three years old at the time of John T.'s death, the second of what would eventually become ten children born to my father and his brothers, Jackie and Barr. Evelyn, now the matriarch of the clan — we all called her "Donna"— continued to come down as usual every year to await those few weeks in March and April when the family would gather there during their children's Spring vacations. I lived the furthest away in Spokane, Washington, and in the early days the trip still took two days. I made my first visit before I could walk, and my parents placed me in a makeshift crib on the veranda until I was old enough to comprehend my surroundings. After I learned to talk Dad would take me on long tours of the island, showing me all the secrets he had learned as a boy growing up there.

My earliest memory is of the sand. It was white, pure and fine, an ubiquitous matrix, which got into everything, between my toes, in my crotch, on my hair and between the sheets of my bed. It covered the paths and was mixed with cement and accumulated in the straw floor mats. Walking around on it was like mushing through foam rubber. When it was dry it was loose and unmanageable, but when wet it coagulated, turning into a rough clay with which I could build sandcastles with moats and arches, miniature forts with dozens of tiny windows poked with a stick out of the agglutinated sandwalls.

The sand teamed with life, especially crabs. There were minute sandcolored crabs, which lived at water's edge and pinpricked my skin in angry retaliation whenever I went wading at night. Larger "sidewise" crabs scooted around in fast-frame action looking for food amid the brown Sargasso at tideline, bivouacing down holes they dug between meals. Hermit crabs trekked through the duned deserts above waterline searching for vacant shells, and seagulls possessively strutted around at the far end of the North beach, dive-bombing me whenever I approached.

At night Dad and I would lie on a beach and star-gaze. He would tell me there were more stars in the sky than grains of sand in the whole wide world, and I would pick up a handful and try to count the grains in a vain attempt to comprehend the immensity of the universe. Then I noticed the sand wasn't really white at all, but made up of millions of blue, green, brown, red, orange and yellow flecks. Dad would explain that the sand consisted of dead crushed shells and pulverized limestone, mashed by waves against the reefs and each other until they disintegrated. At the east end of the island, where it was oldest geologically, he pointed out the fossilized brain corals and conchs embedded in the dark, weathered limestone and told me they were more than a million years old.

The sand, he would say, was at the nexus between the life and death of the island, bonding together under tons more sand on top until it metamorphosed into rock, forming the foundation for a renewed island. The thought worried me; I feared the sea would pulverize the island, and when I built my sandcastles and stood atop the beach dune I would pretend I was the keeper of the sands.

Like many others in my family, I became obsessed with Treasure Island. It was unique, an incredible toy that only we were lucky enough to possess, and each trip to the island was the highpoint of the year for me. I loved to play pirate when my cousins came down, and we would spend hours defending the island from an imaginary fleet of galleons moored menacingly offshore, straddling the rusty cannon next to the cut or hiding behind the tower battlements peppering longboats with musket shot and hot oil if they dared try to storm the cut. Sometimes we caught prisoners and locked them in the tower, just as John T. did years before, hollering and whooping around the base until our parents would call us from their positions across the lagoon where they were quietly painting or reading. Then we could claim the battle was won and trudge wearily up the hill for lunch.

Occasionally we hunted for sharks. Around sunset Wilfred or one of the men would throw out a heavy baited line off the north side. Then we would retire for the night, hoping by the next morning to have bagged a whopper, but invariably we pulled up the line only to find the thick wire had been cut cleanly in half by some night monster. Each sunset I would play taps with my cornet, silhouetted against the waning light while Josephas would lower the flag from the pole next to the Main House. And when the ritual Sunday sing occurred, I would lie on some overstuffed pillows under the dining table, singing along if I knew the words until, exhausted from a hard day's play, I would fall fast asleep and Dad would carry me off to bed.

When it was time to return home Josephas would sing the island "Goodbye" song that was sung at the end of virtually every visitor's stay. Wilfred and I would cry while he hugged me in his black, brawny arms and promise we would meet again next year. A fair percentage of the guests ended up in tears at the words:

Shake my hand and a goodbye
God almighty going to bless you
Shake my hand and a goodbye
For you is goin' home.

Mister (the guest's name), you goin' to leave us.
God almighty goin' to bless you
Shake my hand with Jesus
For you is goin' home.

Back at my fifth-grade classroom at Hutton Elementary in Spokane, where my father had followed John T.'s footsteps as a political cartoonist, all my alabaster compatriots would gather around and fire curious questions at me.

"Well, we have this place that my grandmother owns…" I would start off.

What sort of place? "It's an island in the Bahamas…"

Does anyone else live on it? "No…"

Just you? "Just my family, yeah…"

And you own this whole island? "Yup…"

Wow!

evelyn and josephas

The bills were scattered around the corner table in front of her like so many dead leaves. Evelyn picked up her list of chores from under the latest Bayshore Marina bill and scanned it quickly. Whitewash the cisterns, clean the kerosene lamps, repair the broken chairs, plug up the leaks in the Main House roof, get the south cottage toilet running again, bail out the leaky *Mayaguana*.... the list was endless. Josephas was to have finished most of them by now but Henry Taylor, the latest second man, had quit in a huff yesterday when she refused to increase his meager salary. Josephas was in town trying to scare up some new help. He was supposed to have been back by now and she figured he was on another one of his drunks. She sighed quietly. Lineth would see to Josephas, she knew. Lineth, the best cook the island ever had, would definitely make sure her husband would be ready for work tomorrow.

It had all been so easy when John T. was alive. She wished he were here to help her, but she knew he would probably suggest letting someone else take care of it. Once, when she told him there was $3,000 missing in the account, he suggested she look under the rug and went back to his drawing. John T. never was very good at keeping an eye on the tab.

Until World War II, the cost of running the island had hovered around $5,000 annually, and now in only fifteen years since the war the expenses had nearly quadrupled. Wages had skyrocketed, as had the cost of supplies and equipment. John T. had earned enough of a salary to justify the expenses, but he was a cartoonist, not a businessman, and the few investments he had made hadn't done well. Treasure Island had provided the family with a veneer of wealth that allowed entrée into high social circles; but underneath it was at times a struggle to maintain both the island and the primary home in Lake Forest.

Renting the island seemed to be the best way to raise the necessary operating funds, but Evelyn was hesitant to give it out to just "anybody". The island was a delicate place that required an exceedingly careful, self-reliant renter. A careless elbow could tip over a lighted kerosene lamp; knowledge of boating was essential; the quaint living conditions — a fresh water shower was a bucket poured over one's head — repelled many potential renters accustomed to more luxurious accommodations. Obviously, any renters would have to have already been acquainted with Evelyn and approved by her. Several cautious feelers were put out among her circle of friends, but few even nibbled at the invitation.

She thanked God for John Marquand. The author was the perfect renter, having known the family for years before he began renting the island for a month or so each year just before World War II. He loved the place almost as much as the family, and his rent money had become vital to the annual budget. She hoped he, or his son John

Jr., would keep renting it, and she worried that if he didn't she would be forced to find new renters who might not like the island's quirky character, not to mention the occasional inconveniences.

Sometimes movie people would come around wanting to shoot scenes on the island. Walt Disney wanted to bring over 200 locals from Nassau to film a portion of "Twenty Thousand Leagues Under The Sea," and Ivan Tors once asked her if he could store porpoises in the lagoon for the shooting of "Flipper". Although the money was attractive, she had always refused, not wanting Treasure Island to become another tourist attraction.

Evelyn picked up the Bayshore bill demanding a large amount for repairs on the *Mayaguana*, which had replaced the second *Lucaya* as the primary island tender. The boats were the only mechanical items on the island, and for good reason. Decades of experience had taught her that one of the secrets of island living was to keep everything as simple and machine-free as possible. Rust spread like mold over everything metal, rendering devices such as generators and gas pumps inoperable within months unless properly maintained. She couldn't afford to hire a good mechanic so she had limited engines to only the boats. Water for the bathrooms was pumped manually every morning to overhead tanks, and the propane stove and refrigerators needed only occasional simple maintenance. But even those were becoming a problem.

Jessica Tandy, the actress, had once asked her advice on how to maintain a tropical residence she had purchased on an out island. Evelyn told her to keep everything simple and easy to repair. The actress had ignored the advice, installed air conditioners and a completely electrical kitchen, and the last Evelyn had heard, most of the appliances had broken down and Tandy had sold the place.

Her thoughts wandered back to Josephas. Since Solomon's departure the island's agents, preoccupied with other concerns, had limited their chores primarily to paying the bills and wages, leaving Evelyn and Josephas to pick up the slack. Together, the two of them kept the island functioning and over the years had developed a strange but close bond.

Finding good staff was always one of the most difficult aspects of owning a private island, especially when the bank account wasn't especially full. Josephas and the island agent hired many assistants, but as employment in Nassau was more lucrative and few wanted to live in isolation much of the year, it grew harder and harder to find good people.

Most employees came and went uneventfully, but occasionally some departed with a bit of added drama. One man, a quiet, capable man named Clegghorn was found one day by Josephas floating face-down in the lagoon. He had been working alone on a boat and no one knew exactly what had happened; perhaps he hit his head or had a seizure of some sort. But his was the only death ever recorded on Salt Cay.

Josephas himself had joined the staff in 1929 as one of Levi Glass' assistants, taking over when Levi retired. Maybe Levi was too strict; he had certainly run a taught ship — his fierce, unsmiling visage, his Ghengis Khan mustache and his way of loping purposefully around the island frightened the entire staff into an efficiency unheard of before or since. Maybe it had been too much for Josephas, for he had turned to drinking and almost got himself fired a few times. But he was also an expert sailor, astonishing everyone with his ability to thread those lumbering Bahamian sloops through the narrow cut in a heavy sea at night while so drunk he could hardly stand up. He stopped drinking one night — or at least slowed down — when God was revealed to him in a dream. The Lord, he said later, had scolded him for his wicked ways and told him to shape up, although Lineth knew that at the time he was suffering from a particularly bad case of delirium tremens.

Whatever the cause, Josephas stopped singing those wonderful old Nassau ballads and henceforth sang only spirituals. He attended church regularly, joined the Masons and reduced his binges to only one a month or so. By the time he retired in the early 1970s he had served the McCutcheon family for over 40 years, longer than any-one else, with a mixture of self-serving craftiness and divided loyalty between God, the bottle and the family.

Evelyn wondered again what had happened to her caretaker. He had certainly improved since he found the Lord that delirious night, but he still had a way of "talk-ing with two mouths," as her maid Frances used to say. Marquand had once written a little essay about him and Evelyn thumbed through a pile of papers to find it. Then she sat back and read a section, needing a little reassurance.

"Josephas has a suavity, a charm and ease of manner that I have wished I might imitate. He is humble but he knows that he and I are equal in the eyes of God and he knows that I will understand his problems. He wants to do everything right when I am on the island because he loves Mrs. McCutcheon who does not manage very well and underpays him now that Mr. McCutcheon is gone.

He knows that I will understand, as Mrs. McCutcheon does not, that he has constant miseries in the stomach which more often than not prevent his going out to set the fish traps and spear lobster, although those were his duties. He also has a mother in Exuma who is ninety-three and nearly blind and no doubt the dear old lady is still alive in Georgetown at the moment, at least in Josephas' imagination. Josephas knew from the first moment he saw me that I loved my mother as much as he loved his, and he always knows that I will let him leave the island for ten days, taking ship to Exuma and return-ing, so that he may see his old mother in her last illness — which occurs seasonally just when work is getting heavy. It is true that Mrs. McCutcheon has forbidden him to leave the island for which he is responsible, and he has promised not to do so on his word of honor, but he knows that I will explain to Mrs. McCutcheon the exigencies of the situation, and also why he must go to Nassau for a day once a week for medical attention because of the misery in his stomach, although he has promised Mrs. McCutcheon not to do so.

I am sorry to say Josephas is inaccurate about almost everything. For instance, he has told me that iron-bound chest which stands in the living room of the old house was dug up near his own quarters and that he beheld this exhumation with his own eyes, whereas I know very well that it was given to Mr. McCutcheon by his father-in-law. He also tells me that once when Edward, Duke of Windsor, visited the island in his capacity of Governor, he sang the Duke a song whose refrain goes, "Love, love, love alone; Love made Edward leave the throne." I know very well that Josephas would not have dared do such a thing, and Josephas knows I know, even when he tells me the Duke laughed, fit to die.

In spite of there being at least a thousand bearing coconut palms on the island, there are never any coconuts, as Josephas knows very well when I ask him to get me a green one and lop off the top with his long knife which he calls a cutlass. It seems that every coconut on the island was destroyed in the hurricane last summer, or that a strange new blight has appeared that has prevented the coconuts from bearing. Josephas and I know very well that no hurricane has hit Treasure Island since 1929 and that the coconut palms are in excellent condition. We both know very well that Josephas has harvested and sold all the coconuts in Nassau at sixpence apiece and that he is going to do it again and again. Occasionally, however, I have been able to catch Josephas out on matters like a missing bottle of rum, and on these rare occasions he is most disarming. He hangs his head and bows in defeat and says in a soft voice, "Oh, boss, please forgive me." He always makes me feel that forgiveness is a 'must'; and that night, without my asking, he appears with his guitar when the lanterns are lighted and supper is served on the back veranda.

Evelyn put away the manuscript and chuckled. Marquand had captured Josephas well. She recalled one year when Ernest Hemingway's brother, Leicester, had stored a small barge in the lagoon. Hemingway had been looking around Nassau for a place to put it when Josephas appeared and offered his services. He asked if it was all right with Mrs. McCutcheon and Josephas replied, a bit huffily, that he had full authority on the island when she was gone. So Hemingway put the barge down at the far end of the lagoon, paid the caretaker $90 for three month's rent and headed back to his home in Jamaica. Periodically Josephas would write Hemingway and ask for some extra cash, explaining he needed to pay for his poor brother-in-law's funeral.

Josephas would have gotten away with it had not the barge sunk in the lagoon a month before Evelyn's arrival. He wrote a frantic letter to Hemingway to get his barge out of the lagoon, adding please not to tell Mrs. McCutcheon about the rent money. But the barge was still there, wallowing in the mud like a waterlogged buffalo, when Evelyn arrived. Apoplectic, and not knowing how to reach Hemingway, she placed an advertisement in a Nassau newspaper asking he remove it or be charged for its demolishment. Hemingway wrote back explaining his arrangement with Josephas. Now she was furious with her caretaker, but didn't haul him on the carpet until a month later, after the barge had finally been removed. He hung his head in shame and apologized again and again, knowing that despite the tongue-lashing, she would never fire him, or even dock his salary. He knew very well how to handle Evelyn.

She looked at her watch again and blew out the

kerosene lamp before heading to bed. It was after 9 p.m. and Josephas still hadn't shown up, but she knew he would come in sometime during the night. The next morning it was cold with a northwest wind. Josephas appeared at the breakfast table looking a little bleary-eyed and said he was sorry for being so late. Gruffly, Evelyn accepted the apology and read from her work list some jobs that needed doing. After he left she went down to the South Beach for a quick dip and was walking back when she met him throwing dead palm branches on a large, long mound of them next to the beach for a breakwater. Josephas started in on one of his usual long-winded sermons, suggesting he might like a raise.

"You know, Josephas," she interrupted, "I've noticed how more and more the island was sharing your services with the Lord — how much, I don't know — but wasn't it possible that the church was remunerating you for your excellent preaching?"

At that he flew into another one of his tempers. "You has a wicked and dirty heart!" he yelled at her. "Yes, Madam, you has a wicked and dirty heart!" Evelyn hurried off before he could say anything more.

She found Lineth up in the kitchen and reported the incident, telling her to tell him to apologize. Later he appeared in the living room to ask forgiveness, but instead expressed exactly the same idea in slightly more Biblical terms. "Josephas, you are not talking to me as a gentleman should address a lady and his employer," she scolded him.

"Madam, I can say no less even if I have to leave the island."

"Then you'd better go."

Josephas stomped off, shouting "Come on, Lineth, we's packin' up."

A while later Evelyn went into the kitchen and found Lineth working quietly as usual. Josephas was packing up, she told her. "By and by you'd better smooth him down again," said Evelyn. She went back and spent the rest of the morning puttering about, measuring the water in the cisterns, readying an old table from Van Winkle's time for Josephas to fix and cutting out a new slip-cover for the Gloucester hammock on the side porch. Presently she heard a knock on the door. There was Josephas, standing meekly with tears streaming down his face (Crocodile? she wondered). He held out his hand and she took it.

"The island needs both of us, Josephas. Let's get going," she said. And as they fixed the table, cleaned up the lagoon beach and hung a new tire on the pier he apologized over and over and said whatever arrangement about money was all right with him and that he would never, never leave Treasure Island.

The Mayaguana, *our last Bahama sloop, in the lagoon on a calm day. Beyond, the tower and the cut.*

Josephas Munroe, our Bahamian caretaker, with his guitar. After Josephas no one wanted to work on the island, so we hired Haitians.

Evelyn McCutcheon, the matriarch of the island. She split each year between her Lake Forest, Illinois, home and five months on the island each winter until her death in 1977.

The interior was crisscrossed with concrete paths shrouded by thousands of coconut palms. Here, the path into the interior past the guest cottages.

The path to the South Beach (now the site of a dolphin pen.) Each year the family planted 200 coconuts, and it is estimated there were 20,000 palms on the island by the late 1970s.

The tower with a pirate flag.
The two metal baskets atop poles
were supposed to hold flaming
coconuts to signal for medical
help from Nassau. The system
was never used.

A cousin, John McCutcheon,
steering the Mayaguana out from
the cut. The boat was steered
most easily while standing,
leg against the tiller.

The Custom House
on the southwest
side. Used for
decades as the
main entry to the
island, it fell into
disrepair when
smaller boats that
replaced the large
sailboats could
squeeze through
the cut.

The Mayaguana *entering the cut. With only 2-3 feet to spare on either side, the entry on a rough day could be quite dramatic, especially at night.*

Entering the lagoon through the cut. The 14-foot-wide opening had been created in the late 1800s, letting in the sea to what had been a malodorous salt marsh.

Dawn in the lagoon. The outboards next to the pier changed the way life was lived on the island. Suddenly Nassau was easily accessible.

Bali-Ghit-Ghit, a small courtyard down the hill from the Main House, was one of the most romantic places on the island.

The table set for dinner in Bali-Ghit-Ghit. Lit only by Japanese lanterns and candles and serenaded by the rustling palms, it was a favorite place for meals.

The Balinese statue that John T. brought over from Asia still stands in the center of the courtyard.

The north porch of the Main House, facing the 40-foot-high cliff on the north side. Often the family would gather here for late-night candlelit talks.

Without electricity on the island, kerosene lamps and flashlights provided all the island's light. Here, kerosene lamps wait to be trimmed.

The North Corner of the Main House. An "Aladdin" kerosene lamp used here provided the same light as a 20-watt bulb.

The eye of Hurricane David passed close to the island. Here, 90-mph winds whip up small wavelets in the near-perfect lagoon anchorage.

The limestone outcropping in the distance was called "Nun's Point." Here, a normal day, as viewed from the Main House cliff.

The same scene during Hurricane David. The reefs provided a natural barrier from the waves.

Decades after they were drawn by John T., whimsical pirate art still adorned the interior of the Custom House. The stanchion on the right was an original piece from the U.S.S. Constitution, "Old Ironsides."

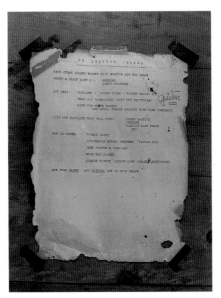

A notice taped by Evelyn on a closet wall gave instructions for closing down the island at the end of the season.

at the boat, she shuddered and went up to unpack.

She had good reason to worry, for the yellow boat, as it was called, changed everything. With this one single item Treasure Island joined the 20th century, suddenly providing a speed and mobility to which the rest of the world was already accustomed.

The yellow boat took only 20 minutes to get into town, less than half the time it took the poky old *Mayaguana*. Diving and fishing trips were transformed into simple, quick affairs, unlike before when such expeditions required half the day just to get there and back. The grocery store was now only minutes away, enabling last-minute runs just before dinner to fetch some eggs. If someone needed to make a phone call he could just hop in the speedboat, whip into town and be back in time for lunch. The staff could run in on Friday mornings, pick up their paychecks and still have enough time for a half-day's work, although they tended to dawdle a little in town. For the rest of the family this new freedom was intoxicating, and the *Mayaguana* was soon relegated to the status of a little-used supply boat.

A couple of years later the family purchased a larger, brand-new twin-hulled fiberglass boat with two outboard engines. No one ever got to use it, though, for a week after it was acquired, one of Josephas' assistants got roaring drunk and rammed the still-uninsured boat onto a reef. The startling loss convinced the family it would be cheaper henceforth to buy secondhand boats, since no one was sure how long they would last. By then, moreover, some family members had begun using the island in the summer months as well, and the outboards just weren't able to withstand six months of punishing use by a dozen different drivers. The engines needed frequent maintenance and the boats themselves, not meant for such heavy salt-water use, rapidly fell apart.

The next boat was a worn-out, patched-up Glastron. It lasted a few years until one afternoon Barr heard someone shouting for help outside the cut. He went out in the Glastron to investigate and discovered a boat full of tourists had swamped just off the island. Some were swimming around the sunken craft while others clung precariously to the edge of the island. Barr began picking up the tourists and had about six in the boat when he noticed water inexplicably splashing around on the floor. Within two minutes it, too, had sunk and everyone, rescuers and rescued alike, had to swim for shore. The *Mayaguana*, good ol' reliable, was dispatched to take the tourists back to town.

Another outboard was purchased, but it was meant more for calm fresh-water than sea duty. Within a year the vicissitudes of rust, coral shoals, concrete seawalls and a sinking or two had transformed the sleek craft into a stale jalopy. The horn hemorrhaged, bleeding orange rust all over the bow, the push-button auto tilt for the engine malfunctioned, the plastic cover for the glove compartment fell off, the back of the driver's seat came unhinged, pushing an adjoining seat out of its socket. The rusty 18-gallon gas tank sprouted a half-dozen leaks just after it had been filled. When the red and green bow light fell off someone replaced it with two chrome automobile taillights, both red. It disintegrated within a couple of months, adding another splotch of rust on the nose. Yet despite all these problems, the family never went back to the old ways. They were hooked.

The outboards brought a new, unexpected problem, too. While they unfettered those on the island, they also unleashed hordes of tourists, brought out in boats rented by the dozen in town for a cheap fee. They came in droves, lurching through the cut to ogle the lagoon, swamping near the beaches as they tried to get ashore, wandering through the interior festooned with Instamatics and eight-millimeter movie cameras with which they took snapshots of their kids lounging on the hammocks. It was as if the world had invaded the family's living room. In one week alone island boats rescued seven boatloads of tourists, caught either on the island or just offshore when their motors conked out.

When the Arab oil embargo happened in the early 1970s, the maintenance and fuel costs rose so much that most of the boat rental agencies went out of business. By then, however, a new type of trespasser appeared: Bahamians grown wealthy off the tourist dollar who could afford boats of their own, and tanned, macho locals who took tourists water skiing and sightseeing, sometimes including the island on their tours. Unlike the tourists, they knew that any beach was public property up to the high tide line, and they would swagger up to the line and dare you to kick them off. There was little the family could do except glare menacingly at them and hope they would leave.

Weekends were the worst. At such time the sea around the island looked like an overcrowded California lake: sailboats, cruisers, speedboats and fishing boats lay anchored offshore like so many gnats waiting to pounce. Various approaches were devised to keep people off, and local mapmakers were asked not to include the island. The most common tactic was to inquire politely, "Can I help you?" Usually they said no, and then it would be explained that this was a private island and that the numerous "No Trespassing" signs they passed on their way in were meant for their benefit. If that didn't work the caretakers were summoned, sometimes being asked to bring machetes just for effect.

Occasionally some of the younger generation would confront the trespassers stark naked. In the old days nude bathing was confined to the South Beach, where a sign could be put up which said, "Stop, Listen, but DON'T Look." By the sixties, however, some of the more liberated grandchildren were romping all over the place in the buff.

I recall one family disembarking from their rental boat onto the lagoon pier — four kids and a couple of parents. They headed up the path towards the main house, toting cameras and a picnic basket. I'd been sans clothes for six days straight and I was getting rather used to it. Other than the caretakers (who didn't count) there was no one else on the island, and when I saw the trespassers walking up the Main House I simply walked up to greet them. For me, the entire island was the equivalent of my own living room, and I had the same proprietary feeling. Plus, I enjoyed their reaction.

"Can I help you?" I said with the cadence of a maitre'd.

Sudden stares, a bit hostile. The woman shooed the children down the path while the man tried to explain. "We were just looking around," he said lamely.

"Well, this is a private island. Maybe you didn't see the signs next to the cut on your way in?"

"Sorry. We didn't know. We'll leave right away."

And the trespassers hurried down to the boat, flung off the lines and sped out the cut. Nudity was often the most effective way to get rid of the interlopers. Eventually the news about his practice reached Nassau, and one day we read an article about the Bahamas in a major travel magazine. Sure enough, there was a reference to an unnamed out island near Nassau that sported a nudist colony.

The final blow occurred one hot summer afternoon while everyone was away on a diving trip, leaving only the caretaker and his wife on the island. In all the years the family owned Treasure Island no one had ever bothered to shut a door except to keep out the wind. Locks were non-existent during the season and buildings were left wide open to cool the interior. That afternoon, as the family left the cut they noticed a small outboard idling alongside the edge of the island as if waiting for someone. When they returned a couple of hours later the living room had been turned upside down. Seat cushions were thrown all over the floor, bureau drawers had been opened, books had been flung from their shelves and several hundred dollars, hidden under a mattress, was missing. No one felt quite as safe on the island after that.

chapter thirteen
hurricane

A t first it was just another unnamed tropical depression east of the Windward Islands. Within a few days, however, the storm had reached hurricane strength and the National Weather Service in Miami gave it a name — David. It was the fall of 1979, and there were three of us on the island, myself, my sister Laurie and a girlfriend of hers. We listened curiously to news reports of David's course as it tore through the Caribbean, waiting to see if it would turn towards the Bahamas.

The last real hurricane to hit the island was in 1965, but the largest and most damaging one, which old-timers in Nassau still talk about, was the Great Hurricane of 1929. For three days and four nights the storm, packing enormous winds, squatted over the Bahamas, wreaking havoc in its path. On Treasure Island it blew away the old thatched Custom House, the South Beach bathhouse, all the summerhouses and about a hundred palm trees. After the storm a massive "rage"— a term Bahamians use to describe sudden heavy seas in an otherwise quiet, sunny day — set in, washing water over almost the entire island. Levi had to climb up trees to avoid being swept away.

David appeared to be just as large and powerful as the '29 storm. We bought a map of the Caribbean in town and began tracking it, using coordinates provided by a Miami radio station. Slowly it moved northwest over Puerto Rico, then turned westerly towards Hispaniola where it hit with the greatest fury. Winds up to 150 mph tore into the Dominican Republic and Haiti, killing a hundred and leaving thousands more homeless. As it moved on we thought it might miss us and hit Florida instead, but over eastern Cuba it turned north, right towards us. Cousin Corwen, Barr's daughter, was due to arrive in a few days to fulfil a dream of spending some time alone on the island with a boyfriend, something she had never done before. It was becoming apparent the hurricane would louse up their plans.

We decided to stay on the island during the hurricane. The Main House had been constructed with such storms in mind and the twin rows of clipped casuarinas around it and the low roofline served to break the winds and actually push the roof down instead of blowing it away. I was more excited than fearful; the Main House had withstood without damage the 1929 hurricane, up until now the century's most severe storm in the Bahamas. And if we had enough food and supplies we could eat well for a week or more. In truth, the island was probably safer than in Nassau; there was less to come loose and blow around.

On a clear sunny morning two days before David hit the Bahamas I went into town to consult with Josephas on what preparations to make. He had retired several years before, being replaced by Joseph Johnson and his wife, Sheila, both Haitian refugees. Neither Joseph nor Mitchell, our Haitian second man, knew what to do. Along the waterfront in Nassau store employees were nailing up storm shutters while marina workers were busily moving drydocked yachts to make room for more boats in the parking lot.

Back on the island the men had begun closing all the storm doors and windows, nailing boards over them to make sure they wouldn't blow open. The windows in the Main House didn't have shutters so we nailed planks inside and out to prevent them from rattling, which Josephas said caused most of the breakage. He also warned us we could be trapped on the island for up to a week, so later in the day we headed back to town to stock up on food and kerosene.

On the way out we met Tony Maillis, an old friend and charter boat captain who for years had acted as unofficial watchdog over the island. He came out frequently with charters, and the family used him as a mailman. Whenever he was out our way he would deliver mail and telephone messages, sometimes shouting the messages from his boat over the roar of the surf. Occasionally he helped repair the island boats and took the family diving and fishing. An erstwhile singer who once aspired to be an opera star, Tony would sing tenor arias over the sputter of his engine while we reeled in mackerel and jack. In return for these favors he was permitted to bring tourists onto the beaches, completing a valuable symbiotic relationship. We asked Tony that morning before the storm to come out as soon as possible after the storm and check up on us. If he couldn't get through the cut we could shout to him our status from the edge of the island.

The main chore was preparing the boats. Three thick hawsers were tied from the *Mayaguana* to two large anchors, while a third anchor was secured north of the boat since we expected the winds to shift from west to north. All the other boats were pulled up on shore, tied to trees and extra anchors in expectation of a large storm surge. Tables and chairs in the grove were moved to high ground and the furniture around the Main House was brought inside. Finally we plugged up the cisterns to keep the fresh water supply from being ruined by salt spray. Then we sat down to wait.

The radio said David would strike Nassau around noon Sunday and the eye appeared to be headed right at us. Early that morning we awoke to slate skies and a stiff breeze. Around 9 a.m. a torrential downpour soaked the island for about a half-hour, slacking a bit later to a steady shower. By noon the gusts had reached 50 mph; this was the leading edge of David. The radio announcer said the rim of the eye was veering slightly to the west of us and was packing winds up to 90 mph — considerably less than several days before.

The old portable tent John T. had brought back from Africa had fallen apart several years before and had been replaced by a similar canvas and screen structure. Realizing it had never gone through a hurricane — the old portable was always dismantled — Joseph, Mitchell and I grabbed some rope, nails and a ladder and headed down through a fierce horizontal rain to tie it down as best we could. The roar of the storm made it difficult to talk while we lashed the roof down to palm trees, which themselves were swaying crazily. A palm frond blew by us as Mitchell stood on the ladder to fix the ropes, braced by Joseph to keep from being pushed over by the wind. The flimsy sides of the canvas tent bent in from the wind, and water cascaded down from the roof, through the flimsy walls and onto the wood floor. The rudimentary fix completed, we leaned into the wind and headed back to the Main House.

Late in the afternoon the old woodpecker tree at the head of the cliff, which had become one of the most venerated symbols of the island, was blown over the winds. It had survived countless storms, hundreds of woodpecker holes and bullets from Navy frogmen. I had been under it only five minutes before, photographing the storm during a lull in the rain. Now the top half lay across the path, its dying fronds whipping in the wind, right where I had been shooting. It seemed an omen.

The storm continued to boil around us; the rain came down in slanting, gusty sheets, pounding the corrugated fiberglass roof in the kitchen with such force and noise it was impossible to speak over the din. Laurie, her friend and I decided to take a tour of the island, making a rule never to go out alone, since coconuts and debris were flying dangerously through the palm groves.

We set out along the paths heading west, planning to walk around the lagoon to the tower. Overhead, we could hear the howling and see the treetops whipping back and forth above us. Oddly, we felt only a slight breeze — it was virtually calm enough to light a match-along the interior paths. It seemed the canopy of trees were so thick that the wind was pushed up and over the island, leaving pockets of calm underneath.

The eye of the storm, meanwhile, had shifted course.

Instead of coming directly at us as we had expected, the eye was moving to the west, between the Bahamas and the United States. Instead of starting from the east and shifting to the north, the wind was coming from the south and gradually moving to the west.

We continued our walk around the lagoon to the stone tower, climbing up the circular staircase to the top. The gusts lashed at the tropical forest, which whipped back and forth like a vast field of grass. The surf on the windward side careened against the reefs and island walls, sending billows of spray thirty feet into the air before the wind caught it and mashed the foam into a fine mist that floated across the interior. On the leeward side the waves were rather small, blown flat from the force of the storm. In the center of the lagoon below us the *Mayaguana* moved quickly around at its mooring, pointed into the wind like a huge weathervane. It looked suspiciously low in the water. I realized it was slowly sinking under the torrent of rain. It had to be bailed out, but all the boats were on shore. There was no choice but to swim out to the submerging boat.

As night began to fall we struggled back to the relative safety of the Main House. I grabbed fins and mask and went down to the lagoon pier. A frothy, two-foot chop — the biggest waves I'd ever seen in the lagoon — marred the normally glassy surface. Bullets of rain stung my skin as I donned my gear and slid into the warm water off the pier. It was actually a relief to be in the water; the chop wasn't bad and I was protected from the machine-gun attack of wind driven rain. The water was so stirred up it was virtually opaque, and I couldn't see my hands as I swam through the chop to the boat. I reached the side of the boat and checked the anchor lines. All three seemed to be holding up well. With a kick of my flippers I hoisted myself up onto the *Mayaguana*.

Inside the cabin the water was above the floorboards; I looked for the switch to the automatic bailer and flicked it a couple of times. Nothing happened. I unhooked the wires leading to the switch and put them together. The bailer began to whir, and for 20 minutes I sat holding the wires together while the boat gradually emptied.

Returning to the Main House, we decided someone would have to go out every three hours and bail it out until the storm was over. I would alternate with Joseph and Mitchell. Obviously no one was going to get much sleep that night.

All night long the storm raged outside. Laurie sat in the North corner of the Main House, a cozy nook in the living room, ears glued to the battery-powered radio for news reports that were now coming in at 15-minute intervals. There were reports of flooding and power outages in Nassau, but in the casino on Paradise Island it was business as usual.

The caretakers remained in their own homes, while we stayed up in the Main House. Occasionally they showed up to see if we were all right, and when it came time to empty the boat again we all traipsed down to the pier with flash-lights to guide the swimmer out.

By dawn the storm had begun to subside and the sun came out briefly. To the north we could see the tail end of David, long streamer clouds bending around the horizon.

Smaller puffball clouds organized in long regular lines zoomed overhead as if trying to catch up with the Mother. With the caretakers we made another tour to inspect for damage. Happily, there was little. We found only eight trees had fallen, but there were palm fronds, casuarina branches and pine needles scattered everywhere. The tide had not come up as far as we expected and the boats were still in place on the beach, although they were all filled with rainwater.

Around noon a heavy gale, formed in the wake of David, appeared from the south and recharged the seas, forming tornados, which damaged several sections of Nassau. In the lull between the storms we began unlatching the doors and putting the furniture back out. Suddenly we heard an engine in the lagoon. It couldn't be, we thought, as we ran down to the pier. But sure enough, there was Corwen, unloading her bags from a tiny Boston whaler. She and her boyfriend had flown in the day before, the last flight to land before the airport closed, and they had spent the night in a local hotel watching boats sink in the harbor. She had found a marina employee willing to take her out to the island for a stiff fee the next morning. Corwen, who was about to fulfill a lifelong wish, was damned if she was going to let a little thing like a hurricane stop her.

the sale

The year was 1977. A chill mid-November wind picked up the few remaining dead leaves from under the massive old elms in the back yard, tumbling them along the ground until they lodged in small piles along the split-log fence. Inside the musty old Lake Forest home Evelyn, now 83, carefully sorted and catalogued the last of her husband's papers in preparation for sending them off to the local historical society. The long tedious job was about finished, and she stood up to stretch her legs. She sat down again quickly, overcome by dizziness followed by a slight pain in her chest. She called Jackie at the Tribune, where he worked as editorial page editor, who drove up and took her to the hospital. Two days later Evelyn died in her sleep of a massive heart attack.

For years the family had debated whether or not to sell the island but had always held off so long as Evelyn was alive and still able to make the trip to her beloved Treasure Island. With her death the debate intensified. The cost of maintaining it had risen to over $20,000 annually, more than the family could bear, and an advertising campaign to find more renters had not produced much results. As the family expanded, squabbles ensued over scheduling, and while on the one hand the island served as a bond among the clan, it also became the subject of minor clashes.

Furthermore, the Bahamian government was beginning to turn anti-foreign as it tested its muscles following independence in 1973. The legislature had passed a stiff new property tax on islands owned by foreigners, which would vastly increase the taxes once a new assessment was made. Too, the trespassers were getting worse again.

Still, Treasure Island was special, a priceless jewel the family had owned for 63 years. It had been a constant in our lives, always there, always the same, our grandfather's legacy. His three sons, upon whom the final decision about the sale now rested, had grown up there, and it had been a focus for clan gatherings in later years. While some of the grandchildren were unable to use it much — some couldn't afford the cost, others couldn't stand the tropical sun — those who could developed almost as intense an emotional bond to the place as their parents. Nobody wanted to think about what life would be like without the island.

In February, 1979, while my parents, Shaw and Nancy McCutcheon, were briefly sharing the island with two renters, Marquand's son John and author William Styron, a German businessman in a rumpled business suit named Ludwig Meister walked up to the Main House where post-breakfast coffee was being served. Several days before, one of Meister's employees had delivered a message that he would like to talk with someone about purchasing the island. As it was not yet on the market no meeting was arranged. The family had already received several other offers, either spurious or too low and nobody figured this one would be any different.

As Dad took Meister off to the north porch to discuss

business, Styron turned to Mother. "Don't sell it," he implored. He had begun renting the place several years before and enjoyed its primitive charm and near-total isolation from the rest of the world.

"Not unless he's got a bundle," she joked. Everyone knew that sooner or later someone would make an offer the family couldn't refuse.

"Wait for me. I'm going to get a bundle soon," Styron said. At the time he was putting the finishing touches on his soon-to-be bestseller, *Sophie's Choice*, and he and Marquand wanted to buy into the island and turn it into a writer's colony for part of the year.

Meister was a developer who had just moved to the Bahamas from Germany, where he had made a fortune in the retail business. From his house in Nassau he could see the island through the Narrows and when he heard that Evelyn McCutcheon had died he was determined to purchase it. He had big plans: condominiums down at the west end, where the island widened briefly; a marina in the lagoon, single-room bungalows around the edge with a common restaurant where the Main House stood. He knew Paradise Island functioned with its own water and electricity and he saw no reason why it couldn't also be done on Treasure Island.

Sitting on the edge of a white slat-board chaise lounge on the north porch Meister made his offer. It was about the same as the others we had already rejected and Dad was noncommittal, saying he had to talk with his brothers before replying. No more was heard from the German until mid-May, when he traveled to Chicago to make a larger offer to Barr, giving the family two months to respond. The new figure was considerable and close to the maximum the family had concluded they would be able to get. The Styrons were contacted to see if they wanted to make a counterproposal, but they could come up with only a fraction of what Meister was offering. The Styron deal seemed attractive but it would have meant a whole new way of life, sharing the island with another group who might have different priorities. Who would use it, and when? Who would pay for the continuing maintenance, and how would it be divided? The questions of shared ownership were endless and without answer. If the McCutcheons later decided to pull out, it seemed easier to sell the whole place than just a fraction.

On June 30 the elder McCutcheon brothers decided to go with the Meister deal, and October 1 was set for the closing. It was a sad, nerve-wracking day for my family, the end of an era. All week long tension had risen in the various households, spilling over into occasional tears as each accepted the inevitable in his or her own way. The Styrons were equally depressed. They had tried to stave off the sale with cash offers and promises to pay the expenses, but Meister's offer was just too large to turn down.

A week before the closing some of the clan came down for a final visit, trickling in by twos and threes. Barr and his wife spent most of the time alone on the beaches, trying to take advantage of their last weekend on the island. Dad, who had never swam from Chub Rock — a scabrous rock in the sea a half-mile northeast of a rocky point on the island — made the effort in 19 minutes, twice the time he figured.

The night before the signing a bottle of 1971 Dom Perignon was uncorked in honor of the last meal, and the family sat around the dinner table remembering the way it was, trading stories, laughing sadly and singing the old island songs. Dad put on a tape of one of the Sunday sings, then had to leave the table when he was unable to choke back the tears.

On October 1, as the dawn broke over a cloud-patched crimson sky, the soul of Treasure Island shuddered in an anguished display of magic. Sometime during the night, without warning and for no apparent reason, the green speedboat which was to take the brothers into town for the signing sank quietly at its mooring. It was discovered resting peacefully on the bottom of the lagoon, the loose seats, cushions and gas tanks floating in the water. No one admitted sinking the boat, and in the emotion of the moment it seemed better to guess that the island itself had done it. For a few moments again the sale was forgotten as everyone pitched in to bail it out. When it was refloated Joseph towed it into town behind the *Mayaguana* to have the engine flushed out, returning later to take the three men in for the signing.

Meanwhile, in another odd coincidence, rock recording artist Keith Emerson was just finishing a happy rhythmic instrumental piece which he titled "Salt Cay," later including it in his solo album "Honky". In those last years he had come over frequently to visit, and on one occasion he dreamed up the basic tune. He was just finishing the final mixing, falling asleep at the recording studio controls, about the same time the boat was sinking.

By the time Joseph got back to the island most of the family was waiting on the pier, their bags packed for flights home later that day. Jackie's wife, Susan, wanted one look at the casino on Paradise Island while the others were at the attorney's office, so Joseph tried to land the sloop near the arched bridge connecting New Providence to Paradise. Just as he was getting close to shore he ran the boat up on a sandbank. Dad and Barr rolled up their pants, got in the water and helped push it off. And so, when they finally arrived for the signing, two of the three brothers wore wet, dirty trousers for the ceremony. It was a typical way to end our association with Treasure Island.

epilogue

Everyone has gone. I have been alone on the island for two months now, having stayed on to write this book and to help Meister adjust to his new possession. It rained last night, a gentle, cleansing shower, and before the bright sun dried it out the island glistened, smelling sweet and pure, touched with the fragrance of jasmine. Today the air is warm and humid and absolutely still, the sea board-flat and a white metal mist shrouds the horizon. The palm forest is motionless, except for a single frond high up on one tree which, moved by some phantom draft, twitches rhythmically as if possessed by a nervous tic. It is the final gasp of summer, the hot, wet season when the cicadas buzz, land crabs forage, birds nest in the casuarinas and the jungle blossoms in a rich green tapestry.

Within a week or so the winds will shift and occluded fronts will blow from the north, signaling the change in seasons. Then the crabs and lizards and insects will retreat for the winter under warm blankets of dead leaves and the birds, unable to find enough food (or maybe they're just spoiled?) will begin flocking to the breakfast table for another helping of sugar or guava jelly. This time, however, I wonder if there will be anybody around to feed them.

Normally there is a steady dull roar of the surf, and you

can sometimes feel base-octive shocks reverberating through the body of the island like a distant cannon as waves punch gouged-out overhangs. But this morning the tranquility is almost complete, broken only by the tickling sound of wavelets, twittering birds and the lonely sputter of an engine as a fisherman in a green dinghy, a fish trap precariously balanced on the bow, prowls the glass water off the north side.

A large hermit crab has crawled into the living room where I write, inching up the leg of the wicker chair, along the arm and up to the top of the back, where it is possessively perched. A banana bird swoops in through a door and lands atop the kerosene lamp next to me, issuing forth a quick little chirp climaxing in exuberant song before darting out an open window. A giant Erebus moth clings to the dark cloth-covered wall, resting during its long journey from Canada to South America. Sometimes they'll sit on my arm and extend their long, tubelike proboscises to slurp up droplets of sherry that I dribble down to them. They love sherry and although I know they've had too much to drink, they always seem able to fly in a straight line.

Everything on the island seems more intense, as if each scene, each object, has taken on a slight glow, like a light-bulb that briefly grows brilliant before fading out. The Main House looks the same as always, the guest cottages are just as comfortable and the sand still shifts around on the beaches, although there seems to be less and less of it these days. (Dad once said he realized the island would someday be gone when the sand in the Grotto, a little cave beach on the north side that was John T.'s favorite, mysteriously disappeared one year and never returned.)

The round carved table, its top a single slab of Philippine mahogany, still dominates the living room, but it seems a little more delicate, more ornate than I remember. Never has the white ceiling, enameled so many times, reflected light with such evenness. The pine posts appear a little sturdier than I know they really are, for in spots I can see where the termites have finally, after a century of trying, made some inroads. The north and south corner nooks have never felt so cozy; novels, magazines and games clutter the recessed window shelves while above them ancient shells, glass fishing net balls and sponges collected decades ago seem a little dustier in front of those distorted leaded windowpanes. And the moldy, worm-eaten books in the bookcase, held together with shiny black tape, appear a little more decayed.

Above the decrepit brown tool bureau across the room is a wall full of relics from an earlier age, gathered by a romantic grandfather with a twinkling sense of adventure. A pirate's cutlass and scabbard, the latter so old it falls apart at the touch; a single-shot dueling pistol in a similar state of disrepair; a coconut carved into the fierce countenance of a pirate, unseeing through a bandana and with two tiny white urchin skeletons for eyes; four small sea scenes with French lettering underneath, painted by someone named Guy Arnoux; two straw fans from God knows where. In the center is a naval map of New Providence, cooked nut-brown from the sea air.

Last night I went diving with a flashlight in the lagoon, inspecting the pier roof again before going in. A bolt of lightening had struck it during the sale negotiations, knocking some shingles off and splitting one of the wooden posts. It was the first time in over a half-century that lightning had hit the island and some said, not unreasonably, that it was a sign from an angry John T. The water was womb-warm as I swam out to the middle. Normally the black void where the light doesn't hit frightens me a little, but last night it was the darkness of safety, of familiarity. Turning out the light, I could see thousands of sparks from phosphorescent plankton swirling from my arms as I swam. Then a tiny worm in front of me died spewing out a bright green phosphorous spiral containing thousands of eggs — the next generation — as it fell to poetic oblivion. Next to the pier, just as I was getting out, the beam of light fell on two tulip shells mating, their muscular feet wrapped around each other in an aquatic embrace.

It is at times like this that the island magic is the most eloquent. Although I am alone, and fully expect to be until I finally leave in a few weeks, I have wanted to share these last days with someone. Perhaps the island felt this desire, for just the other day a girl appeared quite unexpectedly on the porch. She seemed to come from nowhere; I didn't know her at all, but she stayed for a couple of days and has helped ease the pain I know I will feel at the end. She plans to return and spend those final days with me, and although she is very real, I catch myself wondering if she, too, isn't another gift of the island's, part of the enchantment that surrounds it like a halo.

One black night, for example, this girl and I were returning from Nassau under a blanket of clouds. Normally

I run the speedboat with all the lights off, the better to see the vague outlines of the island. But the clouds had obliterated all remnants of light and I was virtually blind, driving only on instinct. But as we approached the cut an opening appeared in the clouds ahead of us, letting through a bright cone of moonbeams, which shimmered on the water. The cone of light merged with us as we neared the island, following us and lighting our way as we went through into the lagoon. A minute later the clouds closed again and the light vanished. The girl laughed afterwards and said she was the siren of Salt Cay.

Then there's Meister. Technically the island isn't his yet; although the papers were all signed the necessary approval from the Bahamian Government has delayed the actual transfer. Sooner or later, we know, the approval will come and then the last gossamer thread linking our family to Treasure Island will be cut. Meister may have to develop the place since the government is trying to discourage speculation by forcing developers to begin construction within a specified time period. But yesterday, while his guests wandered around, he came up to talk. I had expected him to discuss potential development problems: the best place for a restaurant, where to put generators and water tanks, whether heavy rages and storms could ruin new construction, or the most practical way to re-align the cut, which he wants to widen.

None of that, however, interested him. "I vould like to get some information from you about how to operate dis island," he said in his thick German accent. "I have some friends in Germany who vant to rent it — dey're on de

German soccer team, do you know dem? Dey are fine people, I know you'd like dem. But anyway, if I rent de island to dem I need to know some tings, like how many maids do you normally need? And does it take dem a full week to clean up de place after renter have gone? Are de stoves in good working order? Is Sheila a good cook...?"

Meister kept firing more questions, wanting to know everything about how to run an island. When he finished he stood up, thanked me, and walked out to the cliff. Curious, I followed him a few moments later. Maybe this island had cast its spell over Meister, also?

"You know," I said, "if the government forces you to develop you're not going to be able to rent it out much."

"I know, I know. But dis place gets more and more beautiful every time I come out here. It's fantastic. I've never seen anting quite like it before. Day may make me do work on it, but maybe, just maybe, dere might be a way to get around it. Ve'll see."